S0-BEW-299

Epstein   Lend Me Your Alphorn

Cover design and illustrations by Hans Kuechler

Eugene V. Epstein

Lend Me Your Alphorn

Further Tales of Life in Switzerland
By the Author of
Once upon an Alp

Benteli

For Maud, Debbie and Michael

© 1977 Benteli Publishers, Berne
Layout and printing by Benteli Inc., Berne
Printed in Switzerland

ISBN 3-7165-0134-4

Contents

Cyclodrama

When I first visited Switzerland some years ago, I enjoyed walking. This had less to do with athletic inclination than with my personal financial status at the time. I simply preferred walking to starving, and if I had spent more money on riding around the place, I would have eaten less. This may sound complicated to those who have never led the free, easy life of a student in Switzerland, but to me it was a question of pure economics.

As I slowly began to climb life's ladder rung by rung, I soon obtained my first conveyance: a gleaming Swiss bicycle. It was a fine bicycle, and it served me well, even though I was rather uncertain of myself in traffic. At night, I parked my bicycle in a little alleyway next to the house where I lived. In the morning it was still there, sometimes covered with a light dew, sometimes not.

But the point is, it was *always* there. I occasionally locked my bicycle in the beginning, but after a while I didn't bother anymore. There were two reasons for this: first, I wasn't so convinced that such a simple lock on the back wheel would discourage a genuine bicycle thief; and, second, the lock eventually got rusty and ceased to function properly. I was shocked that a Swiss bicycle lock would ever get rusty, but when I examined it, I discovered that it was manufactured in Liverpool.

I was concerned at first that someone would walk – or ride – off with my beloved bicycle, once they discovered it was not locked up for the night. But it was always there in the morning, covered with dew (and sometimes not).

The question of why that bicycle was always there in the morning began to fascinate me. Could it be that the Swiss were just not interested in stealing bicycles, or was there a special Swiss law which was especially hard on bicycle thieves? I began to experiment.

One day I bought a book and left it on the carrier on the back of my bicycle. I left it overnight, and it was there in the morning. I left it the next night, and it was still there. I left it a third night. When I looked for it the next morning, it was gone. "Happy days!" I exclaimed to myself. "The Swiss are indeed capable of stealing things!"

But then I noticed the book on the pavement behind the bicycle. It had simply grown tired of all this experimentation business and had fallen off its precarious perch on the bicycle carrier.

I began to worry about the Swiss, to wonder just what was wrong with them. I studied the newspapers to see what other crimes these perfect people were likewise not perpetrating. My favorite newspaper at the time was the *Neue Basler Bratwurst* – for I was living in Basle – and it had a small daily section dealing with crime.

But, in all honesty, there were very few crimes of any importance, with the exception of an occasional murder or two, most of which seemed to occur in intimate family circles.

I continued my experiments. The book on the bicycle soon became a pound of coffee, which was also still there in the morning. I added a small bottle of whisky, and it too was there – untouched – the next day.

"Ha!" I thought. "I'll catch these super-people at their own game. I'll provide something for them to steal that will tempt their perfect little souls!"

I went out and bought some artificial jewelry: a few strings of pearls for two francs and a rather genuine-looking pair of gold earrings (two francs and forty centimes). I placed them carefully in a paper bag, with a small string of pearls hanging out, and put the whole collection on the carrier of my bicycle.

I could hardly sleep that night. What scientist can rest in the midst of an important discovery? I had a strange, disquieting feeling. Would the jewelry be there in the morning? Did I really *want* the jewelry to be there or would I rather

9

have it disappear? In other words, did I want to lose my faith in the Swiss people and demonstrate – once for all – that they were as human as anybody else, despite some theories to the contrary? I tossed and turned and eventually dozed off.

I awoke when the dawn's early light entered my room. I dressed as quickly as I could and rushed down to the alley. My heart was pounding and I was out of breath. The bicycle...the bicycle, where was it? There...there...against the wall, where it always was in the morning. It was covered with a light dew – as it so often was. But there was nothing on the carrier in the back. My jewelry was missing. Oh joy! My jewelry was missing! Or had it simply fallen off?

I looked underneath my bicycle. I looked all over that alley. It was gone! Filthy criminal, you have absconded with my genuine family jewels! How can one ever forgive thee?

I went upstairs and prepared my usual austere bohemian breakfast of eggs, bacon, cheese, steak, waffles, cake, coffee and ginger ale. As I was musing on this successful conclusion to months of planning and experimenting, the telephone rang.

"Hello," I said into the mouthpiece.

"This is the police department," came the answer. "My name is Dr. Lombardo P. Funderli of the Lost and Found Department, Valuable Stones Division, and we've just received a package containing jewelry which ostensibly belongs to you. Are you missing something or other?"

I told the man I would be right over. When I arrived at the police station, Dr. Funderli explained that one of the good citizens of Basle had seen a package on the back of a bicycle in an alleyway near where I lived. Upon closer examination, Mr. Basle Citizen discovered that some pearls were peeking out of the bag. Our anonymous friend quickly removed the entire package from the bicycle and brought it to the police station.

"That's very thoughtful," I remarked. "But tell me, how did you know the package belonged to me, and that I had forgotten it on the back of my bicycle?"

"Elementary, my dear sir," said the policeman. "We sent a squad of detectives down to the scene of the crime to investigate. They examined the bicycle, checked with the manufacturer, took down the serial numbers of all vital parts as well as the number of your bicycle license. The evidence clearly pointed to you as the owner of said vehicle."

"Are you going to imprison me for my laxity and sloppiness?" I asked.

"Of course not!" said Dr. Funderli. "But we are

going to return your jewelry to you, which, as it turns out, is completely worthless trash. However, you will have to leave a voluntary contribution of, say, five francs for the Good Citizen who meant so well. In the future, please be kind enough to wear your jewelry rather than leaving it sitting around on old bicycles covered with dew. And, furthermore, don't *ever* again try to lose anything in Switzerland!"

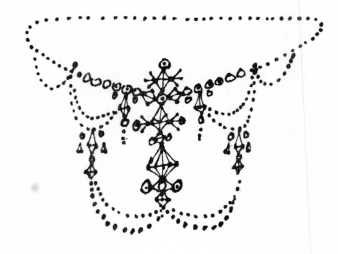

"Ikon"ography

Almost everybody knows where Zurich is, and most people can usually find Geneva, Lucerne and Berne – even in the dark. This is probably what attracted me to Switzerland and why I first visited the country, so many years ago, during my turbulent student days. But I never found the village *I* was looking for, despite the fact that everyone claimed it was so terribly simple.

This particular story begins in a small town in the United States, when a friend of ours suggested that I visit his relatives in a small village near Zurich, Switzerland – which I understood was not far from the Swiss capital of Stockholm. Since I was in any case planning to spend some time in Zurich, our friend said it would be nice if I could deliver his personal greetings from the New World, sometimes known as God's Country. As I was just beginning to write a book on the social habits and sex mores of Switzerland, I was eagerly looking forward to my first real contact with the Helvetic people. After all, if one merely skims the surface, what earthly value can travel have?

I remember quite well what happened during my second day in Zurich so very long ago. I remember rushing down to the main railway sta-

tion and asking for a ticket to the small village my friend had mentioned. At first I couldn't find the crumpled slip of paper he had given me.

"Please hurry, sir," said the ticket agent. "Other people are waiting."

"Ah, now I have it!" I said. "Please give me a ticket to – uh, I'm not quite sure how to pronounce it – a ticket to Dättlikon."

The ticket agent stared at me rather curiously and asked if I was sure of the name. "Of course," I replied impatiently. "One ticket to Dättlikon – first class, of course!"

When I looked at the ticket he gave me, I noticed that the destination was spelled a bit differently than on my crumpled slip of paper: D-ä-l-l-i-k-o-n. But this probably made no difference at all, since I already knew that strange things occasionally happened in Switzerland.

But the conductor on the train seemed confused, too, and, after scratching his head a few times, he told me to get off at a place he called Dietikon. When I mentioned that I was also beginning to get confused, he suggested I try Dietlikon. And if that shouldn't work, he proposed I start with Dintikon, Dottikon, Dänikon and Däniken, and then work progressively through the alphabet. Actually, the first question he asked was if I was sure the name began with "D", because there were thousands of "ikons"

15

beginning with the other twenty-five letters of the alphabet.

"I mean," the thoughtful conductor continued, "have you, for example, considered Tänikon and Tenniken, Trüllikon, Truttikon and Trüttlikon? And why don't you study the problem more carefully before you simply jump on the nearest train? After all, Switzerland is a pretty well-organized place, in case you haven't yet noticed!"

He was right. I should have known more about where I was going before going there. So I found my way back to my hotel, optimistically thinking that I would discuss the whole matter with the desk clerk, who was Swiss and would therefore know everything.

I took stock of the situation. I now knew that I was looking for a Swiss gentleman by the name of Heiri something-or-other, who was the third cousin, twice removed – or second cousin, thrice removed – of my friend in America. I was convinced that I would find him on my second attempt. Anyway, this time I was better organized: I rented an automobile and set out for the village of Uitikon, near Zurich, for this is what the desk clerk had suggested.

In Uitikon, I met a carpenter named Heiri, but he turned out to be the wrong one. He was decent enough about the error – considering that

16

I took him by surprise while he was visiting his mistress – and he gave me a new list of villages I should try in order to find the real Heiri. Uiti-kon, he told me, could easily be confused with Witikon, Wiedikon, Uetikon, Uerikon, Ueli-kon, Uessikon, Uerzlikon and Uffikon.

"And when you've finished with those places," he added, "you might as well try Zezikon, Zimi-kon, Zumikon, Zünikon, Zufikon, Zollikon and Zwillikon. And how about Wallikon, Wal-tikon, Welsikon and Wetzikon, of which there are two – one in the Canton of Zurich, the other in Thurgau?"

Now I was definitely in a muddle. I always thought that Canton was in China, which in it-self was soothing, for Cian-Ciao near Tsutsin was no doubt easier to find than my friend's cousin's village in Switzerland.

I thanked the wrong Heiri from the bottom of my tired feet, deciding that I would carry on my crusade alone – for where there is a will, there's a way. As a matter of fact, I discovered during my research that where there's a Willikon, there's bound to be a Waylikon. There was vir-tually no configuration of letters and syllables that the Swiss hadn't already turned into a town ending in "ikon".

What bothered me most, though, was how the Swiss themselves manage to find each other so readily. Or perhaps they don't, which might explain the reaction of the wrong Heiri in Uitikon when I met him with his ladylove.

Now I began to look for the real Heiri with a vengeance. I visited Mörigen, Möriken and Mörikon, passing through Oetlikon, Opfikon, two Ottikons and an Oppikon. I asked questions of passersby in a pair of Pfäffikons, one Pfeffikon and a Pfeffingen.

I tried Hellikon, Hemmiken, Hermikon and Hilfikon, not to mention Hüniken, Hünikon, Hunzikon, Hüttikon and Hutzikon. And everywhere I went, I asked for Heiri. I'm sure I met every Heiri in Switzerland – Heiris two years old and Heiris eighty-four years old. And most of them were extremely helpful, usually giving me new names and new lists to assist in my search for Cousin Heiri of Switzikon – I mean, Switzerland.

I really began to organize myself. This *must* be a bad dream, I thought, for I had made up my mind to find Heiri or commit Heiri-kiri, as the Japanese would undoubtedly do under similar circumstances.

Gerlikon, Gisikon, Göslikon, Gräslikon, Gündlikon were further stops on my tour. Bänikon, Bellikon, Berikon, Binzikon, Bisikon, Böbikon. Then came Bubikon, Büblikon, Büschikon, as well as Büttikon and Buttikon.

I couldn't sleep anymore. I often woke up in the middle of the night screaming things like: "Heiri, Heiri, where art thou for heaven's sake? What 'ikon' do you live in – tell me, for the love of good, sweet Helvetia, tell me which 'ikon' is *your* 'ikon'!" And a mysterious pulsating rhythm began beating through my head as I tossed and turned in my Swiss bed:

Heiri, Heiri, which ikon, what ikon,
Oppikon, Redlikon, Medikon or Mellikon?
Heiri, Heiri, tell me, tell me!
Nänikon? Nebikon? Ebikon? Nossikon?
Whichikon, Whatikon, Thisikon, Thatikon!

It was pointless; I simply couldn't sleep. Perhaps I should quickly run through all the names in Switzerland. Perhaps I would subconsciously choose the right one.

All right! Blast this country! Blast all the Heiris in this world and blast the Swiss, too – just because they live in such a perfect place. Why don't they do something constructive, such as abolishing all towns ending in "ikon"?

All those Isikons, Islikons, Itzikons and so on. And such places as Landikon and Lendikon, Lachikon and Lutschikon! I mean, for God's sake, what kind of country is this? Anybody who thinks he can find Heiri should go right ahead and try! Why not begin with Ringlikon and

Rümikon and Rumlikon and Russikon? I'll make an exception with Rüschlikon, because Johannes Brahms once lived there, and, anyway, they called him Hans, not Heiri.

Many years have since gone by and, to tell you the truth, I'm still looking for Heiri, with or without mistress for all I care. My list has now been cut down to the barest essentials. There's hardly anything left on it except Adlikon, Amlikon, Attikon, Auslikon, Eschikon, Eschlikon, Etziken, Ehrikon and Ellikon. Then, when I've finished with those, I intend to try Kefikon and Kölliken, Schleinikon, Schmerikon, Schottikon, Sisikon, Stallikon, Sünikon, Winikon, Wolfikon and Vollikon...Damnikon, Blastikon, Hellikon!

Lunar Landscape

As everyone knows, Switzerland simply hums with activity, and nothing, for example, quite matches the Swiss proclivity for road-building and other forms of long-range construction. It is also quite interesting for the layman to observe, at numerous construction sites throughout the country, how the Swiss build for the ages and how carefully everything is done, lest it – during the next five hundred years – come undone again.

There is a basic recipe for building anything in Switzerland: one needs a shovel, a foreign laborer, a bag of cement and somewhere to dig. This latter requirement may seem to be elementary, but it is in reality the most difficult. For wherever one looks, there are holes in the hallowed Swiss earth – holes filled with concrete, holes inside other holes and holes designed for future use in case they are ever needed again.

With all due respect to other countries, there is nothing quite like a freshly dug hole in Switzerland. Each one represents an unusual combination of beauty, perfection and Swiss quality workmanship. This is certainly why building firms are constantly competing with each other in the fine art of hole-digging.

The trouble with all this construction business

is that there is often no really good earth left in which to dig really decent holes, and the situation is obviously not going to improve in the near future, especially with land prices as high as they are.

Yet Switzerland already seems to resemble a lunar landscape, with crater upon crater signifying that something dynamic is about to happen. During the day, there is a great deal of dust and noise signifying that momentous things *are* happening. Holes are dug, concrete is poured, rocks are blasted, all to the hypnotic accompaniment of diesel engines and expletives in assorted foreign-sounding languages.

In order to dig and pour and blast more efficiently, it is often necessary to redirect traffic. The constant flow of traffic can seriously slow down work on an important construction project, and the point of all the noise and dust and roar is to finish whatever is being built as quickly as possible. Because – whatever it is – it is undoubtedly needed for whatever purpose the voters of a particular community thought it was needed.

The trouble is that no one really understands how complicated and time-consuming building can be. With traffic out of the way, construction foremen and laborers can proceed with the basic problem of pure building. But there are other problems facing these selfless servants of the community. For example, the man who was supposed to deliver mixed concrete in a special truck was delayed by heavy traffic, and his concrete – as well as his truck – hardened along the way. Closer investigation uncovered some interesting facts. The truck was held up because traffic was being detoured around a construction project which itself was delayed because another concrete-truck man couldn't get to where he was trying to get in the first place.

On another occasion, an entire community was cut off from the outside world when construction engineers severed the only road above and below the village. When asked why they cut off both ends of town at the same time, they answered that the voters had approved the two projects but apparently hadn't thought of the consequences. What eventually happened was that a helicopter service was proposed to keep the village from starving to death. The disadvantage of the plan was that there was no place to land in the entire area. "Come, come," said the mayor. "There must be a field or meadow or flat plot of ground somewhere – I mean one that isn't private property." And he went into consultation with the other members of the town council.

"What about Plot 1215?" asked one of the

23

councillors as they all studied the official village map. "Plot 1215 is currently under construction," answered the mayor. "That was last year!" said the councillor.

"Wasn't that the plot where we were going to build a sewage disposal plant?" asked another councillor. "No," said the mayor, "as far as I can remember, we were reserving that piece of land for a new school."

"New school?" said the chairman of the school authority. "We finished our school last year, don't you remember, Mr. Mayor?" But the mayor was obviously confused.

"Oh, now I remember," said he. "The school we completed last year was the one we started planning in 1923, and I'm afraid it was obsolete the day I personally dedicated it. So I gave orders to have it torn down the following Tuesday, because we needed the land for our sewage disposal plant, which, as you know, the voters have already approved."

"Approved or not approved," replied the school chairman, "the fact remains that we have neither school nor sewage disposal plant nor helicopter landing strip. We're surely going to starve if we don't watch out, not to mention what will happen to us if we don't get something fairly acceptable to drink pretty soon!"

When they finally located some flat ground for

the heliport, further difficulties were encountered because it was soft and swampy, and everyone was afraid the helicopters might sink rather than fly, thus depriving the village of all hope – forever. The representative of the building authority – who also happened to own one of the local construction firms – suggested that a project be approved to drain the swamp.

"How can we possibly drain that land if we're cut off from civilization at both ends?" asked the mayor. "Easy," replied the builder. "I happen to have two Italian workers left up here, and I'm sure we can find some shovels and some cement. We'll have that field drained before you can say 'Swiss Family Robinson'."

So they began to dig seven large holes to drain the water. The local surveyor visited the site every forty-five minutes to assure that all was going according to plan and schedule. And when the holes were finished, they were shored up with fresh concrete, and grass and flowers were planted to hide the ugly scars left by such large-scale construction. The field was now dry and seemed excellently suited to support the first helicopter landing.

But one point had been overlooked. The seven new holes had indeed drained the field, but it was now impossible to land a helicopter there because the holes themselves were in the way.

"Well," said the mayor, "we tried, we really did. Perhaps it's better this way – being cut off from the outside world. No more noise, no roaring and pouring, no traffic, no expletives, and, above all, no more hole-digging!"

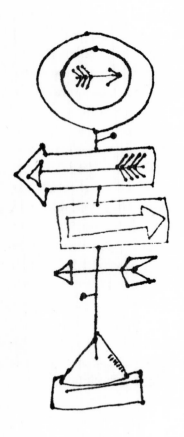

How Many Rolls Did You Have?

Many traditions in this world have become well-established simply because no one has seriously questioned them. As a result, they are treated almost reverentially, and anyone who suggests a change is likely to be labelled anarchistic or, at the very least, anti-Establishment.

All right, then, perhaps I am a mini-anarchist at heart, because I now have the intention of challenging one of Switzerland's most perfidious traditions. Let the chips fall where they may – I am clearly and openly against paying extra for rolls when I eat in a Swiss restaurant.

Everyone knows that Swiss restaurants are generally excellent. It is, in fact, quite the usual thing to use the word "cuisine" when referring to the food specialties of Switzerland. And this is really quite impressive if you consider that the majority of us would be happy if they even used the word "food" in connection with several other countries we know of.

So what am I complaining about? I am complaining about the fact that I am forced to count the wonderfully crisp Swiss rolls I consume during my meal. Then at the end of each and every repast, I am required to state – virtually under oath, with right hand solemnly raised – that I stuffed three or four of them into my voracious gullet. I insist that charging for individual rolls consumed is a violation of human rights and personal freedom, and I intend to take up the matter with the Council of Europe in Strasbourg.

Perhaps I'm just hypersensitive. But I simply dislike informing complete strangers that my body needs so-and-so-many carbohydrates in order to exist. I admit to some degree of corpulence, but this is quite obviously my own business – no one else's. Yet Swiss waiters and waitresses continue to ask me that most insulting question: "Hänzi Bröötli ghaa?" – "Did you have any rolls?"

There are many reasons why I am so fervently against this particular Swiss tradition. First of all, I find it hard to remember how many rolls I have eaten. Then, I find it humiliating to add a few trifling centimes to a bill which may well come to fifty or sixty francs anyway. And, from the business and good-will point of view, what has a restaurateur actually accomplished when he collects fifty francs for a first-class meal, then loses the customer because of an argument over whether he had two or possibly three *Brötlis?* In addition to the fact, of course, that one pays 15 per cent service charge on every last flaking one of them.

The problem, though, has nothing to do with

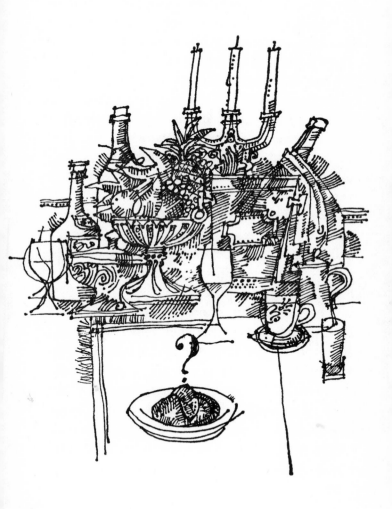

me, for I have lived in Switzerland for a number of years and have some idea of what to expect. What about the poor tourist?

He enters a restaurant and orders a *Wiener Schnitzel* with French-fried potatoes. It could be – assuming that he is American – that he likes ketchup, not only with Schnitzels but with French-fried potatoes as well.

So he orders ketchup, and the friendly waiter nods appreciatively. Our tourist can hardly believe his eyes. Amid all these foreign dishes – Viennese veal and French potatoes – there now stands a bottle of genuine old-fashioned American red-blooded ketchup. It's enough to make a person cry or even to burst out in song.

After singing one stanza of "God Bless America", he proceeds to pour ketchup all over the Schnitzel, the potatoes and his tie. Then he eats, relishing the magnificence and munificence of Swiss quality and quantity.

My mouth waters at the enticing thought of what that tourist is experiencing, perhaps at this very minute. But to continue this tale of gustatory delight, our American acquaintance completes his meal, daintily soaking up every last drop of ketchup with a golden brown Swiss roll. He then washes down the entire mess with a quaff of genuine Swiss apple cider, burps discreetly and asks for the check.

The waiter brings the check immediately, and our tourist studiously examines the hastily scrawled document. After deciphering it, he notices that the ketchup is listed at fifty centimes, or approximately 12.5 centimes per shake and glob. The guest turns red, either because of the vast amount of ketchup in the process of being digested or, more likely, because of the indignity of paying for...for...so help me...ketchup!

"Paying for ketchup!" the tourist thinks. "I'll break the damned bottle over that waiter's square head!" Then, tempering his temper, he calmly asks the waiter about the ketchup.

"Ketchup costs money!" snaps the waiter. "One bottle, one franc and forty-five centimes."

"But I didn't use one-third of a bottle," says the tourist.

"Doesn't matter," replies the waiter. "You could have."

"Had I but known," says our friend, "and I would have emptied the whole thing on the floor! As a matter of fact, I think I will!"

"Sorry, sir," replies the waiter. "This rule comes from the manager, and there's nothing I can do about it."

And so the guest agrees to pay, however reluctantly. He hands the waiter a twenty-franc note to cover the total of twelve francs and sixty centimes, and the waiter begins to count out the change, then suddenly halts.

"Did you have any rolls?" he asks.

"Rolls, what do you mean rolls?"

"Did you have rolls with your meal?" the waiter repeats.

"Of course I had rolls," our friend impatiently groans. "That's what they're on the table for, isn't it?"

The waiter finally convinces his irate guest that such information is important because, not only must he pay for the rolls, but these facts are regularly passed on to the Federal Department of Statistics, not to mention the Foreign Police.

"Okay, Buster," says the exhausted tourist. "I had three. How many million golden Swiss francs do you want for them?"

"Let's see," says the waiter, "three rolls at 50 centimes makes one franc fifty which makes fourteen francs ten total which means you get five francs ninety back."

"Thank you," says the relieved visitor from the New World.

"With service," adds the waiter.

"How very kind of you!" our exhausted American replies graciously.

And so the story goes. I want to stress here that paying for ketchup is quite unusual, except that it happened to me, and in a rather well-known

Zurich restaurant (name available upon request). When I tried to provoke a charge for ketchup during a second visit to the same restaurant, I learned that the place had a new owner, and that ketchup was now included, although the *Wiener Schnitzels* were decidedly smaller. Or perhaps the humidity on that rainy day made them shrink a bit.

In any case, the fact remains that most restaurants in Switzerland charge for rolls, if not for ketchup. And anyone who seriously tries to eat Swiss rolls without accounting for them is making a great mistake, because the crumbs have a habit of sticking to clothing, and you can't dispute such evidence when the police arrive to question you. I know, because I've tried it.

The Great Salt-Bath Controversy

It is quite customary in many European countries to bathe as often as possible, despite what
foreign visitors have occasionally thought.
When I first arrived in Europe – a young and relatively naive American student – I was amazed
at this unusual phenomenon. This was because
Americans, living up to their fabled time-is-
money motto, rarely seemed to have time to
relax in a bathtub. But Americans always have
time to take a "quick shower" (I never heard of
a slow shower), although I really didn't know at
that time precisely why Europeans prefer baths.

I soon found out. Most Europeans take baths
not only because water is wet or because soap is
cheap. They take baths in order to add things to
the water. These may take the form of perfumed
exotic oils, or they may be bubble formulae with
scents redolent of Alpine forests or Egyptian
street markets. The odors are good for one's
morale and self-confidence, while the oils and
bubbles are supposed to be good for the skin, especially when they contain extract of chestnut or
a host of other health-giving ingredients.

And here we hit upon the real reason for baths
in Europe: the health syndrome which pervades
almost every aspect of life on the Continent,
particularly in Germany, Austria and Switzer-

land. Whatever you do, make sure it is considered healthy. In fact, use this as an excuse for doing things you might otherwise consider unhealthy.

But back to baths and how they can improve your life. Excluding the perfumed variety of bath for a moment, there are many other types which deserve mention here. There are sulphur baths, good, so I am told, for whatever may ail you. Sulphur is good for acne and eczema and for the skin generally, but it will invariably result in one's losing one's very best friends, because sulphur smells terrible – and for weeks on end. Sulphur baths can be taken at home or at various spas all over the Continent, as can many other baths containing everything from iron to radioactive minerals.

The most popular bathtub additive for the average European is sea salt, which is likewise said to be good for everything, especially for the people who sell it. Sea salt is sold in plastic bags and in barrels, depending upon whether you want to use it in your bathtub or in your swimming pool. I personally know several people who use tons of the stuff in their pools, with the nostalgic explanation that it reminds them of the sea and is healthy to boot.

No one has really ever explained why bathing in sea salt is so terribly beneficial. On the other hand, no one has explained why bathing in sea salt is not so beneficial.

I intend to explain why, in my opinion, sea-salt baths far from the sea are both frivolous and ecologically nonsensical. Imagine, for a moment, how much technological energy has been expended in the development of practical systems of ocean desalination. Imagine how much money has been poured into this important break-through: how much it will mean for man to obtain his drinking-water from the sea. With traditional sources of fresh drinking-water rapidly becoming polluted, with irrigation so essential in providing sufficient nourishment for our population-exploded world, desalination seems to be one of the answers. Yet what has happened?

Here we have, on the one hand, the people who have learned to extract salt from sea-water. On the other hand, we find other people taking that very same salt and using it to contaminate their bath or swimming-pool water. The fresh water produced from desalination is further purified and piped into homes which never before had potable drinking-water or bathable bath water – and everybody thinks this is marvellous and a really up-to-date "science working for all of mankind" kind of thing. In the meantime, we have all those Europeans dumping tons and tons of salt into their drinking-water, which they admittedly do not drink, but this is merely a technicality. They don't drink this water because they know that too much salt is unhealthy in the stomach, even though it may be quite healthy *on* the stomach. But, in any case, our drinking water supplies are becoming contaminated with salt from our seas, and I personally think it is time that something be done about this unfortunate state of affairs.

I have made a brief study of the entire situation, and I feel the results should be brought to the attention of all interested persons. In the first place, I have concluded that if salt-bathing continues at the present rate, and if the population continues to grow, and if the future population also wishes to relax in sea-water-filled bathtubs, we shall soon find that our inland fresh-water supply has been supplanted by an inland salt-water supply. By the same token, the seas around us will contain less and less of this important mineral. Marine life will become quite confused and many varieties of fish will think they are in streams instead of oceans and begin to swim up rivers in quest of salt water instead of fresh water. It is almost incredible to contemplate what this may mean to the love life of the sockeye salmon, just to take one example.

My study also shows that, as the salt is gradually

depleted in our oceans, tourists will no longer find beach holidays as attractive as they were in the past. Inland lakes will become famous for their saline content and deep-lake fishing, while the oceans will be equally well known for their constant supply of small but edible rainbow trout.

There is simply no end to this sad tale of ecological imbalance. Think of the freight charges alone: moving carloads of salt from the shores of our oceans to inland areas costs millions and millions of whatever currency you care to think in.

Let this be a warning, then, to all those who regularly take sea-salt baths. Think of what you are doing to our already messed-up ecology, and try to develop your own do-it-yourself desalination apparatus for home use. In any case, consider the sockeye salmon and the rainbow trout, and try to let them live in peace. And if you can possibly live without salt baths, why not try sulphur? Sulphur smells more than salt, but it's more beneficial too – especially against acne and eczema.

GRÜEZI
GRUEZI

Grüezi

grüezi

mitenand mitenand

Grüezi, Grüezi, Everybody!

The only thing that confuses me in Switzerland is the idea of greeting everybody by his family name. I realize that – on first sight anyway – this doesn't appear to be so unusual. I also realize that some people would question why this seemingly small matter should be the most confusing thing I have encountered in Switzerland, a country reputed to be confusing in far more significant ways.

I do not want to disparage Switzerland's hard-earned reputation for confusing people, because this wouldn't be fair. But I have spent many years here, and I have come to the conclusion that greeting people by name is one of the most diabolical tricks ever perpetrated on mankind.

I personally have considerable difficulty remembering names – even my own. Perhaps this has something to do with my upbringing in America, where "Hello, folks" and "Hi, neighbor" really suffice as far as the social graces are concerned. But the Yankee form of address is considered almost contemptible in Switzerland, where everybody is courteous, kind, obedient, helpful and reverent.

So the first thing to learn in German-speaking Switzerland is that "Grüezi" is the standard greeting. Except that life isn't quite so simple in my favorite Alpine democracy; otherwise one might learn far too quickly, thus taking the joy and aura of suspense out of everyday living. I suppose everyone knows that "Grüezi" means "hello" or "greetings" or "go to the devil," depending on how one spits it out and on one's tone of voice and facial expression. But – and here's the point – it is considered most impolite to say "Grüezi" without using a person's name along with it.

For example, when you enter your local grocery store, you are expected to greet Frau Stirnimann, the owner's wife. So you say, "Grüezi, Frau Stirnimann," and Frau Stirnimann returns the compliment with a warm "Grüezi, Herr Epstein," if that happens to be your name – which is doubtful. So far, so good.

The trouble with all this "Grüezi-ing" business is that I simply cannot remember names – try as I will. In one way this is good, for I am constantly reminded of my own name when people like Frau Stirnimann keep cackling "Grüezi, Herr Epstein" into my ears all day long. But I nevertheless have a great deal of difficulty remembering Frau Stirnimann's name, and have thus begun to mumble what I consider the approximate number of syllables in a particular person's name.

This is fine as far as it goes – but it is obviously

not the ideal solution. If you mumble "Grüezi, Frau Ungh-hxp-li" when the person you are addressing is named Frau Pfister-Pfammatter, she may well wonder what happened to the rest of her respectable Swiss family background. So I have devised a new set of rules which works in most cases and affords me a certain degree of protection in others.

First of all, I try to frequent grocery stores where there is more than one person on duty. If – as a case in point – Frau Stirnimann *and* Frau Pfister-Pfammatter were theoretically working in the same store at the same time, my life would instantaneously become more livable. Because then I could say "Grüezi, mitenand," which means "Greetings, all together" – and this is quite acceptable, even among the Zurich blue bloods.

But, as a result of my miserable memory, I am forced to sneak up to stores like a petty thief, peering in windows and around corners, just to see whether one or – let us pray! – *two* people are serving the customers. Fortunately I don't have to shop so very frequently, and, anyway, there are still other means of avoiding this uniquely Swiss form of torture.

Incidentally, the "Grüezi, mitenand" technique is also effective if there's at least one customer in the store, in addition to Frau Stirnimann. It even works at my tennis club, where everybody looks alike in tennis shorts and sweaters. So I have no trouble there, especially since I have now learned to distinguish the girls from the boys.

Actually, it really isn't fair to foreigners like me who are doing nothing more than trying to earn an honest living in Switzerland. The Swiss themselves are born with an incredible ability to remember thousands of names. In fact, I even suspect them of practicing some modern form of witchcraft, for they seem to anticipate names before hearing them, and they're *always* right – these Swiss – they're always right and they never forget: a name or anything else!

Having now spent more than a decade studying the social climate in Switzerland, I have added some nuances and sly subtleties to this game of greeting people, wherever they may be. For example, although I prefer to walk alone, I would rather have a person with me who knows the name of anyone we're likely to meet on the street. This person is generally my wife, who has performed yeoman service in remembering all the Stirnimanns, Pfister-Pfammatters and Schuppissers in Switzerland.

My personal specialty is a simple one. If I encounter someone with a title – a doctor or the director of a company – I can get away with a quick "Grüezi, Herr Doktor" or "Grüezi, Herr

Direktor." Now the odd thing about Switzerland – and Europe generally – is that the wives of doctors and directors (and even butchers) may also use their husband's titles. Many years ago, I considered this to be a most undemocratic way of doing things. Now I absolutely love the system, because I can say "Grüezi, Frau Doktor" most of the time and have a fair chance of hitting the bull's-eye. And if the lady in question should not be a doctor's wife, she's usually flattered that I consider her a member of the modern Swiss aristocracy. I mean, it is certainly better to use a title than to forget a name, isn't it? Now of course there aren't *that* many doctors or doctor's wives in Switzerland, but there are more than one would think, especially if we include advertising executives and streetcar conductors, all of whom seem to have obtained doctorates of one sort or another.

Summing up today's lesson in how to succeed in the glorious and picturesque land of Helvetia, I offer the following advice:

1. Try to manipulate people into groups before you greet them, so that you can get away with "Grüezi, mitenand." If you are then asked to shake hands individually with everyone present (and would thus have to use names), mention casually that you are just recovering from a set of broken fingers sustained when you last shook

hands with the Swiss National Wrestling Champion.

2. Use "Grüezi, Frau Doktor" or "Grüezi, Herr Doktor" as often as possible, even when addressing children. The young people invariably like this sort of thing, because it shows that you're not afraid of undermining the Establishment. Or they may simply think you are out of your mind, which is roughly the same thing.

3. Walk three paces behind your wife, if she happens to be as good at names as mine is. When she greets Frau Stirnimann, just repeat it, and you'll get along fine.

There are, of course, additional rules to be learned, particularly for me. For example, I'm not quite certain how to ask my wife to join me for a walk. I obviously can't say, "Would you join me, Frau Doktor?" since neither she nor I are doctors. Nor can I call her Frau Stirnimann, since I generally know who she isn't. I am terribly embarrassed about all of this, because her last name and mine are supposedly the same. Perhaps the only solution is to obtain a doctorate or open up an advertising agency.

The Stamp-Sticking Syndrome

The Swiss are among the world's foremost collectors. They collect art and they collect coins, they collect medieval swords and Alpine butterflies. Many of these pursuits are admittedly limited to those who specialize in certain subjects or simply to those who have the money to buy an extra painting or two. Or, as the local proverb has it, "Money buys Monet."

Now just where does this leave the people, the average Swiss man-on-the-street, the honest, hard-working, good-natured fellow who hasn't got the money, interest or taste to go around buying dozens of Monets – or even Manets? Here, I am pleased to report, Swiss industry has stepped in to fill the gap.

The average Swiss collects points. Points?

Points are sometimes called "checks" and checks are sometimes called stamps. But whatever you call them, they add up to a way of life which is at once diabolical and extremely clever. For example, wherever our average Swiss housewife buys her groceries – with some exceptions – she will receive stamps when she pays her bill. These stamps represent the total amount of her purchase and can be returned to the store after being pasted into a special book. The housewife then receives five or eight per cent of the amount in cash. On the surface this would seem to be a rather decent sort of system. In other words, if you collect 200 francs worth of stamps from a particular store or cooperative organization, you would receive sixteen francs back – after, *nota bene*, you have pasted the stamps into your little book.

Now what's so diabolical about that? Simply that our little stamps are, in fact, often microscopic in size. A stamp representing ten centimes is difficult to see, much less moisten. And don't forget that two thousand such stamps would be required in order to get your ten francs back, assuming, of course, that there were no larger denominations, which there are. However, this is just the beginning of our story, which, I hope, will moisten tongues as well as eyes, for you will need sufficient saliva if you ever want to see your money again.

It would be all right, I suppose, if the Swiss would leave it at this. But, like many things in this land of supreme contrasts, there are vast differences and many varieties of stamps, points and checks. Did you know, for example, that you can improve your general education – as well as the appearance of your library – by buying certain products, saving their special points and sending them in to a certain publisher? If you save, say, six hundred so-called Silver-

Moon points, you can send them in and receive in return a set of color pictures, which you can then paste into a book. Where does the book come from? Never underestimate the Swiss, please. The book comes from the Silver-Moon publishing people and costs only seven francs fifty.

It's actually a most interesting system. The points are found on (or in or under) the packages of various products, the manufacturers of which belong to a particular organization. The books themselves are of high quality and can certainly be recommended. Here, however, I am forced to register a minor complaint or two on the method of collecting these points. For example, you must accumulate six hundred points (plus seven francs fifty) for the average book. Now this may sound like a pretty simple affair for the uninitiated. But do you realize what is actually involved? Let us assume that you wish to collect your points from bottled beverages. One liter of carbonated drink will produce precisely one point.

So start collecting. If you drink one liter a day – which is a lot – you will surely have enough points for a book in slightly under two years, assuming that the cost of the drinks has not left you in abject poverty, because you will still need seven francs fifty for the book itself.

Collecting is really not as bad a pastime as it seems, because it serves to keep the average Swiss out of trouble, which is what the average Swiss likes to keep out of. Forgetting the cost of the drinks, plus the fact that I have exaggerated the whole affair by failing to mention the many other products containing the same points which can be simultaneously collected, what else is there to this sticky story?

If you look carefully, you can find five points on a certain brand of toothpaste, which you will need anyway if you drink all those sweet carbonated drinks for two solid years. Or if you buy thirty deodorant sprays all at once, you would have enough points right there to obtain a set of pictures to paste in a book. Now, what about all this pasting?

The diabolical part of the story is that many of the products you would need in order to obtain pictures and buy books with are sold in stores which themselves offer "Rabatt" – or rebate – points or stamps or checks to loyal customers. And what, you may have the temerity to ask, is a *loyal* customer?

A loyal customer is a guy who buys. Period. Full stop. Many years in Switzerland have taught me – even though I am loyal by nature – that it is not necessary to collect stamps in order to get my five or eight per cent return. The simplest way – without wasting time or saliva – is to ask to have the amount "abgezogen", or deducted, from the bill as you pay. The trouble here is that, in certain Swiss stores, you get looked at as if you were cheap, parsimonious and generally un-Swiss, for the Swiss, as everyone knows, are world-renowned for their extreme generosity.

Thus life becomes quite difficult. First of all, you can't be sure that what you have purchased – for example, in a drug store – is charged on a net-price basis or if a rebate is granted. And even so, you don't really know if the discount is five or eight per cent. If you should decide to accept stamps, you likewise don't know if you can actually use them, particularly if you happen to visit a store away from your own neighborhood.

So you ask, as I suggested earlier, for the amount to be "abgezogen", and you get the usual look, along with the usual comment: "This is our net price."

On the other hand, if you don't say anything, you might end up with a handful of worthless stamps, especially if you happen to be on holiday somewhere in the lovely Swiss mountains.

So you look at the stamps and timidly ask what you're supposed to do with them.

"Do with them?" comes the answer. "Put them in a book, of course!" "But I don't have a book," you reply. "Couldn't you please...uh, madam...deduct the amount from the total bill? You see, I don't live here – I'm only visiting."

Now you may prepare yourself for the Swiss equivalent of a tornado if not worse: "Young man, if you want us to deduct the five per cent, why didn't you say so in the first place and not wait until I've given you the stamps?"

You try to explain that you tried this technique yesterday and that it didn't work – because what you bought at that time was sold at net price.

"Well," the lady will then say, "I can't help it if you bought only milk, cheese and eggs yesterday. These are *'netto'* items. Today you bought Fifi-Cola and toothpaste." Then she adds that these particular items also have checks for pictures which, with the addition of seven francs fifty, will produce a book into which one merely has to paste the pictures.

"Wait a minute!" I say. "You mean to tell me that I have to paste these points into a book and send them in, then I get a book and some pictures which I am then permitted to paste in as well? No wonder the Swiss have to drink so much – a normal human being would be dehydrated by that time!"

"No, you foreigners are all alike – you simply do not understand us! I didn't say you had to paste the points into a book. I said you had to paste the pictures into a book. And that you get the book by *collecting* points, and that you collect the points by buying in my store. Is that clear?"

"Yes, except for the little stamps that started the whole argument. What do I do with them?"

"Oh those," the lady replies. "You paste them into a book of course."

"Which book? The same one you order for seven francs fifty?"

"Of course not, you – you – heaven forbid – I almost said 'idiot'. You paste them in a *Rabatt* book like this one here, then you return the book and get five francs something for every hundred francs something. But make sure you paste all the teeny-weeny stamps in the right places and that you paste only so many stamps per page. After all, you don't expect us to sit around all day counting stamps, do you?"

"How about me?" I dared to ask.

Anyway, that's how it all started when I first became acquainted with Switzerland and its unique customs. Today we collect everything – all colors and types of stamps and points and checks – in an aging shoebox which is kept on the top shelf of our kitchen cabinet. After twelve years, we have collected almost enough Juwo points from eating cream cheese to apply for one five-franc coin.

I have an envelope full of points before me right now, and I'm just going through them. Here is one metallic-looking rectangular green point from an ice-cream package (it seems, from the spot on it, to have been chocolate). Oh, and here's an eight-pointer from a detergent and a beautiful air-freshener ten-pointer (yellow and red). And here are fourteen additional points in eight different sizes and shapes.

And so it goes – on and on. I strongly suggest that everyone collect and collect and collect, for you never know when you might welcome the opportunity to have something to do. Such activity keeps the mind active and supports Swiss industry as well. And, when everything is said and done, don't forget that you will, within the next decade or two, have several very nice books (for seven francs fifty) into which you can paste and paste to your heart's content.

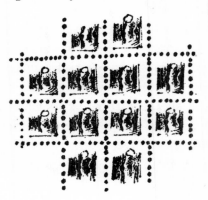

A Tale of Two Sausages

I wonder how many non-Swiss in this world really know what a "Metzgete" is. Yet *Metzgetes* are as Swiss as any of the Swissiest things we've ever heard of, including fondue, milk and money.

Now, just what *is* a *Metzgete* and what's so special about it? First of all, a *Metzgete* is not an "it" – it's a way of life – at least in the German-speaking part of the country.

It seems odd that some of the most fascinating traditions in Switzerland have something or other to do with eating. The *Metzgete*, however, doesn't only have something to do with eating, it has *everything* to do with eating. In fact, it's the heart, brains, lungs and guts of eating. One might even suggest that these are precisely the victuals one eats at a *Metzgete*, but such a thought might frighten away a number of prospective customers from what is generally a very pleasant evening of superior indigestion.

The first time I went to a *Metzgete* I was more naive than I am today, which, according to my wife, must have bordered on the improbable. Some very dear Swiss friends of mine picked me up one night at the little pension in Zurich which was my first home in Europe. This was many years ago, and I therefore ask the indul-

gence of my readers should some of the more sa-
lient impressions of this evening have become
subsequently faded or confused. One thing I do
remember: prices at that time were a good deal
lower than they are today. People are supposed
to be earning more money today, though, so
that everything comes out even in the end. I'm
not particularly concerned about this theory,
mainly because I wasn't earning anything at all
at that time – I was a plain, old-fashioned, un-
hippie-ish kind of student. But, as I recall, I
was nevertheless able to afford all sorts of luxu-
ries. In any case, my tastes were modest and on
the rustic side. This is why I liked my first *Metzgete.*

Walti, my very Swiss friend, arrived at my little
pension with Ruthli, his new girl friend, whom
I rather liked as well. Ruthli was not aware of
this fact, and I managed to conceal my inner-
most feelings by letting her think I came along
because of the fine food we always ate together in such great abundance. (My editor just
telephoned to ask why I never stick to one subject. "If you're writing about *Metzgetes,*" he
screamed, "why the devil don't you stick to
Metzgetes?" He's right.)

Anyway, Walti appeared at the door of my little
pension that evening with a strangely mysterious look in his baby-blue eyes.

"What's up?" I inquired. "Why the strangely mysterious look?"

"In Switzerland," he replied, "we usually begin a conversation by greeting our friends. I refuse to exchange any words with you until you do so. Understood?"

"Okay, okay!" I replied. "Grüezi, goddam it! Now what's up, where are you taking me and, furthermore, where's your horrible girl friend? Can't we ever go anywhere without her? Always around, always sticking her nose into our business. Ruthli this and Ruthli that!"

"Shut up!" said Walti with his customary politeness. "Ruthli's in the car, and we're going to a *Metzgete*."

"What's a *Schwetzgete*?" I asked.

"*Metzgete*," said Walti, "Metz-ge-te, Metz-gete, M-e-t-z-g-e-t-e! Got it now?" A *Metzgete*, he carefully explained to me, was a so-called slaughter festival, which, I still have to admit (as I did then), sounds reasonably disgusting. This is the kind of slaughter affair where an innkeeper butchers up a pig or two and serves the various parts in various ways to various people. Swiss laendler music is played to keep the people from concentrating on what they're eating.

Walti and I and that girl friend of his drove off in Walti's pre-war Mercedes to what a travel agent would describe as a charming, quaint old inn in the country. The area we ended up in was – and is – known as the Säuliamt (or pig's office) which no doubt had some symbolic meaning in relation to our planned *Metzgete*. "Aha," I thought, "this must be where all those Swiss pigs come from."

Säuliamt is simply the name of an attractive area not far from Zurich as the crow flies. In Walti's pre-war Mercedes it seemed to take us most of the evening to get there. Walti always drove slowly when Ruthli was sitting next to him. At first I thought he was merely safety-conscious. When I mentioned this to him, he replied that he just liked girls, especially when they were sitting next to him on the front seats of pre-war Mercedeses.

We finally arrived at the Gasthaus zum Ochsenschwanz – a quaint, lovely, picturesque inn in the middle of a pine forest. Walti parked, wiped the lipstick off his cheek and announced that we had finally arrived. I could hear the heart-warming strains of Swiss laendler music escaping through the cracks in the walls of the Gasthaus zum Ochsenschwanz. I had an odd feeling that something was about to happen to me, something I would be writing about two decades later. I made a note to this effect on the back of a ticket I received that day for talking back to a policeman.

We entered the quaint and lovely inn, and some-how – despite the thick clouds of acrid smoke which greeted us – found our way to a table where three seats were still free. The place was horribly crowded, noisy, hot, smoky and smelled of grease from the kitchen. Our neigh-bors at the table – an elderly, corpulent Swiss gentleman and his wife – had napkins tucked into their collars and their mouths were stuffed. They gasped the standard "Grüezi" as we sat down.

Now what, I thought to myself, can be so unique about so uncomfortable a situation?

The waitress appeared. Walti asked for three Bratwursts, three porkchops, three liver sau-sages and – the most ominous-sounding of all – three blood sausages. On top of this, he ordered side dishes of sauerkraut, potato salad and lots of bread. And then he asked for three large bot-tles of beer.

"What should we order as a main course?" I had the temerity to ask, as we all tucked napkins into our collars. "Enough of your infernal wise-cracks, young man!" said Walti. "Just do as you're told and you'll eventually learn how to get along in Switzerland."

Now, two decades later, I know that Walti was right. We ate and ate that night so many years ago. I realize there's nothing especially romantic about porkchops. And those ghastly, ghoulish blood sausages represent a culinary delight I would prefer not to describe at the moment, since my stomach tends to become upset whenever I think of them. Even the liver sausages would fit into the same category. They come on platters: huge, bloated balloons of sausages waiting to be stabbed with the nearest fork or knife. I sincerely caution all would-be sausage-stabbers to stab carefully and slowly.

I was not very careful that night at the Gasthaus zum Ochsenschwanz. I stabbed at my first liver sausage and a geyser of thick brown liquid shot up at the lamp hanging over our table. But I learned that there is nothing better than liver sausage oozing out all over one's plate. This is precisely why I find *Metzgetes* so interesting. Everything is rough and seemingly primitive – yet good at the same time. The music is loud and noisy – yet it also belongs to the whole scheme of things. The porkchops are sometimes greasy. And they are good, too. The sauerkraut is usually quite tasty, and the Swiss always knew how to make good potato salad.

So, all in all, a *Metzgete* is a most acceptable kind of local tradition. Today I am still fascinated by them, and I have attended *Metzgetes* all over the country. One of the worst took place at an extremely expensive and elegant restaurant in Zurich. The porkchops were exquisite, the sausages succulent, perfectly spiced and well-behaved. The sauerkraut contained carroway seed and champagne. Even the blood sausage was edible, especially if you closed your eyes. But it was a terrible *Metzgete*.

I later learned why. You see, there was no greasy smell emanating from the kitchen and there were no acrid clouds of smoke from dozens of Swiss cigars. The place was simply too fashionable, and, what's more, one never has neighbors at the same table in such elegant restaurants. Perhaps I was also dreaming of my very first *Metzgete*, of Walti and Ruthli, of that battered old pre-war Mercedes and how carefully Walti drove on his way out to the Säuliamt.

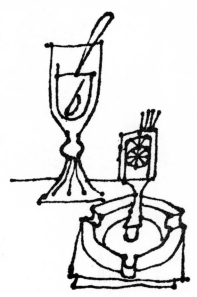

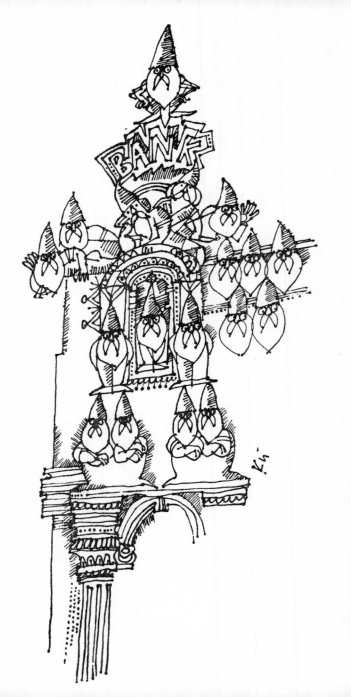

If It Weren't for Berne, Zurich Would Be the Capital of Switzerland

"The apple crates burning on the shores of the Lake of Zurich gave off an eerie glow as the tired Swiss fishermen tied up their boats among the seagulls and restaurants along the lake."

I once read that a well-known Italian author always begins his books with anything that happens to come to his mind. Such as "The orange crates were burning brightly against the hazy twilight."

I suppose I could have begun this piece on Zurich with something about orange crates – rather than apple crates – but I don't know too much about orange crates, except that they're generally made of poplar.

Anyway, there's a special reason for writing about apple crates in Switzerland, for apples are an important symbol in the Alpine country. They have nothing to do with fertility, which exists in Zurich even among people who never eat apples. Oranges, on the other hand, may have a lot to do with Italy, but you can't eat them in Switzerland without first depriving them of their skins and pits.

Apples are a historic symbol, because of William

Tell, who must have seen red when he shot one off the top of his son's head. This sort of sport is now frowned upon in Switzerland, mainly because the Swiss are an orderly, law-abiding people, which makes them quite the exception in this world of violence and fun.

In any case, my introduction and supporting explanation having been completed, I can now proceed to why Zurich is where it is and how it is.

The first reason for Zurich's being in Switzerland is that it's the biggest city and *not* the capital of the country. If it were the capital, the Swiss would have to build a bigger city to not be the capital, because capital cities are always smaller than other cities in their respective countries. I mean, take the case of Washington, which is smaller than Tokyo, but nevertheless the capital of the United States.

Berne is the real capital of Switzerland, which brings us back to the combustible crates we were talking about earlier. One rather famous Swiss (and there are some) once said that we're all going to Berne in the end anyway.

Before beginning this article on Zurich, I would like to dispel one or two fallacies about the place, because I like to be positive, and I've heard that some people have at times expressed negative thoughts about Switzerland and even

Zurich. Particularly about Swiss money and Swiss banks.

I would have to admit – if put to the test – that there's a great deal of Money in and around Zurich, and that a lot of it is kept in Swiss banks, which, as everyone knows, sometimes tell people that bank accounts are occasionally even numbered in Switzerland. This fact came as a great surprise to me when I first heard it, because I immediately wondered how else a bank is supposed to keep track of its money and its depositors. If you don't number an account, I suppose you would have to letter it. And, as my research has proved, there are simply more available numbers than letters.

So, once and for all, Swiss bank accounts are numbered because the Swiss are very orderly and law-abiding, and one particular Swiss book-keeper, in the year 1872, invented an ingenious method of numbering bank accounts. His name was Willi P. Gnome of Zurich, and, as a special honor, he was awarded Swiss Bank Account No. 1. Since that time, a number of other people all over the world have discovered that Swiss banks are orderly and law-abiding and likewise began applying for numbered accounts. I think it was the King of Transylvania who got Account No. 2 – just before he was exiled. This little story points up the importance of Swiss banks and what they do for the small man – the man on the street – like the King of Transylvania. Were it not for his Swiss bank account, the former King would never have been able to live out his days on the French Riviera without fear. Nor would he ever have been able to pay the twenty-seven crew members assigned to his yacht, the "S. S. No. 2".

Because of Willi P. Gnome, the entire banking community of Switzerland soon became known as the Gnomes of Zurich. At least that's the story one hears in London, which also has banks and should know. But the essential difference is that – in London – the accounts are still lettered. I have tried in vain to find out who owns British Bank Account Letter "A", but, for some reason, Her Majesty's Exchequer wasn't prepared to divulge this information. So much for banks.

Zurich is really a lovely city, and anyone who thinks I'm joking should really be awarded a free trip here by the Swiss National Tourist Office, which is usually quite generous with its money. When I put the idea to the Tourist Office people, they agreed with it in principle, but someone there suggested that good photographs might well take the place of a personal visit, especially if they were expected to pay for the pleasure. And, anyway, photographs of Zurich can be taken on sunny days, while visits to

66

the city can happen almost anytime, although the precipitation has been minimal this year.

There is a great deal of vital information I should impart before *really* beginning this chapter, because people read stories for information, not only for pleasure. I wonder how many people know, for example, that the Lake of Zurich freezes over every thirty years or so, and that when it does it's usually during the winter months. And it's quite a sight. I waited here for thirty-two years and three months before the lake decided to freeze over, despite continual prodding by the Swiss National Tourist Office, which likes such things. I guess they feel that it breaks the monotony of day-to-day living in Zurich. Anyway, it breaks the ice.

As I was beginning to write, I waited for thirty-two years and some months and damned if the silly lake didn't finally freeze over. It was late, of course, which sorely embarrassed the Swiss, who are very punctual as well as law-abiding and orderly.

But when that lake froze over, it really froze, which proves the old Swiss proverb, "If you can't do a thing better or cheaper, why do it at all?"

This frozen lake was a humdinger of a frozen lake, and those of us who waited thirty-odd years for this frozen happening honestly didn't wait in vain. That Zurich ice was hard and firm and cold – as good Swiss ice should be.

The second day of the big freeze on the Lake of Zurich, I personally counted 22,456 individual ice skates on the lake. This means that there were 11,228 people out there skating that day. Less one person, I mean, because I had skates on but wasn't really doing very well.

But Zurich has a lot of other things to recommend it besides frozen lakes and bank accounts. It has food, for example. It even has frozen food. Zurich's hot food is considered to be excellent in quality, especially when it's hot and of good quality. There are a lot of restaurants in Zurich, and most of them serve food which is considered to be of excellent quality. One favorite dish here is fondue, which is not native to Zurich, but, for that matter, neither am I. Fondue, as almost every idiot knows by this time, is a melted cheese dish. Now if you've ever tried to melt a cheese dish without a blowtorch, you will quickly realize that this melted cheese dish must really be something. Which it is.

All right – I admit it – I like fondue. I like fondue quite a lot, especially when I have a cold and don't have to smell it. But that doesn't work, either, because people with colds in the nose are not supposed to partake of fondue, unless they eat solo rather than in a crowd. This is because everybody eats out of the same dish, which is an odd state of affairs in a country as orderly, law-abiding, punctual and hygienic as Switzerland. But it has been said that a correctly made fondue will kill any organism known to man, and I therefore don't want to frighten any potential fondue customers away.

And for dessert, there are many nice specialties, including Swiss apple pie, which is as Swiss as American apple pie was originally Scandinavian. I don't think I mentioned this yet, but there are a lot of apples in Switzerland, and – according to the Swiss Apple Growers Association – we really ought to help eat them up. According to the Swiss Cheese Union, we ought to help eat up their cheese, too, especially the holes. But the problem then arises what to do with all those apple crates after we've finished off our Swiss apples. That's why one sometimes sees them burning on the shores of the Lake of Zurich, giving off their eerie glow among the seagulls and restaurants.

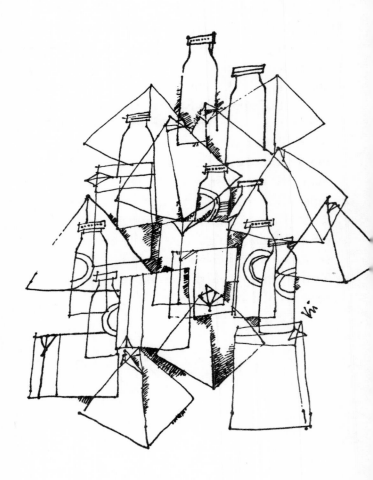

Ali Baba and the Milk

It is no longer customary for a man of my age and social standing to drink milk, but occasionally I get the urge. As a matter of fact, I've always liked milk, and perhaps the years I've lived in Switzerland have influenced me as well. Some of my fondest childhood memories have something or other to do with milkmen, who, in those days in the United States, delivered their fresh dairy products at four in the morning from a horse-drawn wagon. My younger readers will no doubt wonder what sort of antiquated, dated old kind of writer I am, but this happened not so many years ago.

Anyway, the milkman used to come at four in the morning, and the clop-clopping of his horse occasionally woke me up. But it was a pleasant sound – one of security and orderliness – and there weren't, in that era, very many other sounds to wake one up. In the morning, milk bottles could always be found in their special wooden box (with a hinged top which was always warped), provided by the dairy of one's choice. As I recall it now, the milk itself was of especially good quality, easily recognized by the collar of yellow cream at the top.

Though it is difficult to believe, there was a time when cream floated at the top of the milk – and one could see it and knew that it must be good. Sometimes the collar of cream was thicker than at other times. When it got too thin, we used to complain and threaten to change dairies unless they put the cream back in their milk.

When we drank that good old milk, we shook the bottle as if mixing a cocktail, for otherwise one person might get all the creamy cream at the top, while somebody else – usually me – would get stuck with the milky milk. I probably didn't realize it then, but this served as a fine lesson for life itself. I've never forgotten that there are those who get the cream and those who get the milk, no matter how you try to shake things up.

Then they started changing things in the milk business. I neglected to say that milk was pasteurized in those days, but that was all they did to it (I guess). At this point in history, science and technology took over and started adding various things like homogenizing and vitamins A and D. Science also took away a few things, too, like the horse whose clop-clopping used to wake me up. And then, in most areas, they took away the milkman, too. But the milk was now homogenized, and it was supposed to be much better because the cream was *in* it rather than on top of it. And this ended forever the shaking of milk bottles which once belonged to our mornings as much as bacon and eggs.

Soon we were faced with another disaster of more than minor proportions: milk was being sold in cartons, in *paper* cartons! The glass bottle was rapidly disappearing and, with it, more of my boringly nostalgic childhood memories.

These particular cartons were considered very good things indeed – much better than their glass predecessors. They were thought to be more hygienic and, in any case, were certainly lighter to carry. But in the old days we didn't have to carry milk anywhere except from the icebox to the table. Now we had to buy it in a store and carry it home, and, for this most plausible reason, science made everything easier for us – and we mustn't forget the pasteurizing, homogenizing and vitaminizing. But the point of all this is a simple one: even with cartons – which I didn't particularly like – it was terribly easy to pour a glass of milk. One merely had to open a neatly hinged top and pour. When one's glass was full, one simply had to stop pouring, close the top and put the wretched carton back in the icebox.

Chapter two of my milky story begins and ends in Switzerland, where I now find myself a number of years, and a great many incidents, later. The first thing I noticed when we moved here was that milk was delivered to our door every day, including Sundays. There were no horses – for Switzerland is a modern country in every way –

but there were *bottles!* Twenty, thirty, I don't know how many years had passed unnoticed, and we were pouring milk out of bottles again!

Our Swiss bottles were brown, which, I understand, helped to protect the contents (pasteurized and homogenized) from the evil effects of normal daylight. So the milk looked brown but poured white and was delicious. But even those were prophetic days. For as good as the Swiss milk was, the tops of those brown milk bottles were rather silly contrivances. They were made of some kind of metal foil, and once they were torn open, they really didn't fit on the bottle anymore. But this was a minor complaint. I must admit, though, that I would have expected Swiss science and technology to come up with something that would close the top of a milk bottle once it had been opened. I mean, if they think of coloring the bottles brown and all that.

Then, one day, catastrophe struck. The local dairy announced that all milk would henceforth be delivered in cartons. I was confused, for I had been through this business before somewhere else – at least I thought I had – or was it just a normal case of *déjà bu?* When the cartons – which were made in Germany – first arrived, I couldn't believe my eyes. They were fat and had a roof on them, and there was no visible way of opening them. I examined one more carefully.

There was a clever drawing of two ladylike hands showing me how to open the frightful thing. The drawing was accompanied by the words: "Please tear open like this." Meanwhile, the lady was holding the roof of the carton with one hand, the carton itself with the other, and was apparently pulling in opposite directions. Obviously something had to give – so I tried the same maneuver myself.

I pulled and pulled, and the carton began to tear. It tore at the top and it tore on the side. A huge opening appeared out of nowhere. I felt like Ali Baba immediately after he had uttered the words, "Open, sesame!" Anyway, my milk carton was surely open, paraffin was peeling from the sides, while much of the milk was all over the table and dripping rhythmically onto the kitchen floor.

I thought seriously of complaining that I had ordered a bottle – I mean, a carton – of milk, and that when I wanted paraffin I would go out and buy a candle. But this was progress and should not be fought against. The paraffin content of our milk was eventually reduced and I learned to open the cartons – and it usually worked. But my problems were not yet over. There was still the cream to worry about.

Milk and cream, in many parts of Switzerland, came in the form of a tetrahedron – or four-faced, yet triangular pack. And the only way of opening such packages was with a pair of scissors. Since there is no known way of closing them again, we needn't dwell on the subject.

There's even another kind of milk in another kind of carton which looks fairly innocent but is as devilish an invention as anyone ever came up with. Its directions read: "Reach into the fold and pull apart." Try it, I dare you! And do get to know the orange juice which comes in neat-looking liter cartons bearing the inscription "shake gently before using" or "shake before opening." Remember that you must drink either a full liter of juice at one sitting or be satisfied later with a breakfast drink which is either too thin or too thick. Once opened, these Swiss cartons can never again be transformed to their pristine state. Nor can the juice ever be shaken again – not even gently – without splashing all over the furniture.

Anyway, that's the story of my life with milk. What I forgot to mention is that when you pick up one of the new soft cartons – which now seem to be replacing the hard ones – the slightest squeeze forces milk or cream or whatever to squirt out the top, which is never closed once it has been opened. I love Swiss milk, I really and honestly do. But I often think of that old milkman and his horse at four in the morning and wonder whatever happened to them.

Bankseeing in Zurich

Before beginning this story about Zurich, I received strict instructions from an anonymous caller not to devote an undue amount of space to banks or gnomes or numbered accounts.

I wouldn't have anyway, but it's perhaps a good thing to get out of the way at the beginning of a chapter, so that the unsuspecting reader will at least know what kind of an author he is dealing with. I'm the sort of fellow who hates to see this bank thing overdone in Switzerland. Having lived in the country for the better part of many years, I really feel that banks are what people generally write about when they've run out of other things to write about – especially in Zurich.

Now there are those who contend that it's very easy to run out of things to write about in Zurich, "Mainly because the city is really not that interesting, you know." This is a fairly convenient kind of excuse for a writer – and I speak now as a member of the trade who would jump like a shot at a reasonable pretext not to study a subject before writing about it.

The problem with me is that I've lived in and around Zurich for the best part of my active life, and I can tell you right now that it's at least as interesting as some of the other famous cities in this smashing world of ours. As a matter of fact, it's sometimes even more interesting.

As a further matter of fact, what does "interesting" mean anyway – if one stops to think about it? If I would mention at this point that Karajan conducts in Zurich about once every two years, how would that statement affect you, the individual reader? For those who know an infinitesimal something about music, this fascinating fact might produce a mild yawn at best. For those who don't, we might hear, "So who's Karl Jahn anyway? Isn't he the guy who sells grilled chickens all over Europe?"

But Zurich *is* an interesting city, I swear it! The place even has several sights worth seeing, if you'll kindly pardon the expression. I promised my editor to mention some of them, and we'll simply have to start somewhere or other.

The first idea that occurs to me is that the thing most cities have in common is that they all have sights. Can you for a moment imagine a city without anything to see? That in itself would be good enough reason to take a look at it, of course, so why make such a big thing out of looking? More important is *understanding*. I mean, you can look at a million churches, but if you don't know anything about what goes on in churches or who built them or who destroyed them or restored them or painted in them, what good is all that walking around the place looking at stained-glass windows?

Banks, on the other hand, should really interest everyone who visits Switzerland. I've argued and argued with my Swiss friends about this aspect of life in the Alpine democracy, and I always get the same type of reaction from them.

My good friend Walti, for instance, invariably screams at me. "Why do you Yanks always talk about Banks and Francs?"

"I don't always talk about banks, you idiot!" I told my very good friend. "I like to talk a little bit about Swiss banks because people expect me to say something about Swiss banks! And, furthermore, I honestly think that your compatriots, the bankers of Switzerland, will soon begin to develop some semi-super inferiority complexes if everybody goes around ignoring them."

Anyway, that's the reason I thought I would take the liberty of mentioning the fact that there are a number of banks in Zurich. For those of you who plan to stay here for at least five or six days, you will no doubt have enough time to catch at least a quick glimpse of most of the major banks. I would suggest you find your way to the foot of Zurich's renowned shopping and banking street, the Bahnhofstrasse.

If you're lucky with the weather, gaze out now at the Lake of Zurich and at the Alps off in the hazy distance. If you're unlucky with the weather, either carry an umbrella or for heaven's sake stop taking the advice of every travel writer you come across.

Zurich is a very attractive city, right? I think anyone would agree. You know, there are not many cities of this size which look as picturesque as Zurich does. On a warm summer day, the lake is dotted with sailboats and swans, rowboats and gulls, paddleboats and pigeons.

There is a special kind of symbiosis between Zurich birds and Zurich boats. If you look to your left – you're still standing at the foot of Bahnhofstrasse, remember? – you will notice a bridge over a river. The river is the Limmat, the name of the bridge is unimportant. But if you stand on that bridge and look away from the lake – that is, towards the town – you ought to find enough tantalizing sights to electrify you for the rest of your life. The twin-spired church on your right is the Grossmünster, which is supposed to have been built around the year 1100. The fat churchtower on your left is that of St. Peter's, and although I've never been in the church, I do know that the clock dial, which measures quite a few feet in diameter, is the largest in Europe. There's one further churchtower you will notice, also on your left: the thin, single spire of the Fraumünster.

Now let's return to the foot of Bahnhofstrasse and begin walking up towards the railroad station. The imposing edifice on your right just one block from the lake is the Swiss National Bank.

On the other side of Bahnhofstrasse you will see another bank – the Zurich Cantonal Bank. A few steps further and you will reach Paradeplatz, one of the main squares of the city. On your left at Paradeplatz, please notice the Swiss Bank Corporation, one of the three so-called "big banks" of the country. Straight ahead of you is the Swiss Credit Bank. The main entrance, also on Paradeplatz, took on an infamous sort of notoriety not too long ago, because through it passed a woman who deposited a vast sum of money earned, it is said, from an autobiography allegedly written by one of the world's wealthiest men.

And where, would you guess, is the third of the country's big banks? Just keep walking, and, lo and behold, there it is, in all its proper dignity: the Union Bank of Switzerland.

You may find it hard to believe, but I have spared you at least fourteen other banks on your way to the People's Bank of Switzerland, so please don't vent your ire on me just yet.

I simply had to get this off my chest. Since I

have never seen a "Guide to the Banks of Zurich", I decided to write one myself.

Now what else can one say about a city like Zurich? If you ask me, I would write another thirteen hundred pages, but I'm not sure I would mention one solitary sight again.

But that's enough now. I do not propose to ruin your stay in Zurich by giving you any further advice. If you're really interested in the Thomas Mann Archives, then go and find them. If you want to see where James Joyce ate in Zurich, then visit the Kronenhalle Restaurant. By the way, James Joyce is buried in Zurich as well. If you want to find out where, I suggest you ask someone. As a matter of fact, how do you think your hotel concièrge might react if you asked him: "Say, could you please tell me where James Joyce is buried?" Try it and see. (Warning to all Zurich hoteliers: please immediately find out and inform your personnel where James Joyce is buried.)

Now, in conclusion, I would like to add a question which just popped into my own mind. Who the devil is James Joyce?

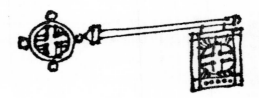

The Bells

I can well remember how hectic it was when we first moved to Switzerland some years ago. Of course, moving is always hectic, which is why it really isn't such a pleasant enterprise for someone as lazy as I. Anyway, I managed to summon up enough strength and energy to help my wife when we moved to Switzerland some years ago, and we somehow succeeded in getting here and ensconsing ourselves in our new home on the Lake of Zurich.

After so turbulent a beginning, I was looking forward to a bit of rest in the fabled peace and quiet of Switzerland. After all, as I mentioned, moving is a strenuous sport, and I've always felt that my contribution to life in general should be limited to the more intellectual pursuits. But now I could relax and look out over the shimmering lake: an almost hackneyed picture of lake-steamers, swans, sailboats and sunsets presenting an ever-changing, picture-postcard view from the apartment into which we had now moved. And I looked forward to sleeping.

Ah! The mere mention of the word "sleep" made my aching bones tingle, for what steak is for the stomach, sleep is for the aching bones. We had spent months and months preparing and carrying out our move (I planned the overall

83

logistics while my wife took care of more mundane things) and sleep was what I now needed. A few days of rest and all our work would soon be nothing more than an unpleasant memory.

At seven o'clock that first evening on the Lake of Zurich, I slipped delicately between the fresh white sheets of my new Swiss bed. It was heavenly. It was in fact so peaceful that I deliberately stayed awake a bit longer in order to savor the beauty of it all. The fresh night air blew into my room through a curtainless window, and I was soon able to glimpse the newly risen moon as it reflected on the waters of the lake. I remember hearing the bells of a nearby church toll eight o'clock, and then I must have fallen asleep.

I dreamt of moving vans and furniture, of customs declarations and residence permits. Then suddenly I was awakened by the loudest and most frantic ringing of bells I had ever heard. There must be something wrong, I thought to myself, for it was only five in the morning. What a strange hour for such a racket! Then I realized that this was no doubt some unique and typically Swiss alarm system and perhaps there was a fire or something in the neighborhood. Those bells rang that morning a total of four hundred and sixty-three times. (I learned only later that this would happen every morning.) While they were ringing, they also set off a number of sympathetic vibrations in my room and in my head, while their cacophonous overtones filled the air with a permanent din.

But when it was all over, I appreciated the quiet even more. It was as if someone had deliberately tortured my ears just to prove how fortunate I was to have silence once again. I rolled over and fell asleep.

Then the doorbell rang. Good grief, I thought, have I slept so long already? I looked at my genuine Swiss watch. Six-thirty? It simply couldn't be, for no one in his right mind would think of ringing other people's doorbells at such an absurd hour!

I was still somewhat groggy from the moving business as I stumbled out of bed. I felt around the floor for my slippers and managed to get into my English bathrobe even though it was inside out. It was still reasonably dark outside and I was in a hurry to find out who was at the door. I had heard stories about early-morning visits from the police in strange European countries, but this certainly couldn't be true of Switzerland. What was that old story about democracies and dictatorships? In a democracy, so it went, when someone knocks at six in the morning, it's only the milkman.

"Of course," I muttered softly to myself, "the milkman, delivering his fine Swiss milk." I opened the door, and there stood a boy of no more than nine years. He was wide-eyed and considerably more awake than I. As my sleep-filled eyes grew accustomed to the light of the corridor, I noticed that he was carrying a huge basket filled with delectable-looking Swiss bread and rolls. How magnificent! Even though I had been forced out of bed at six-thirty, I had the satisfaction of looking at and smelling all those wonderful rolls. There were all the traditional varieties: *Gipfeli* and *Weggli* and *Bürli* and *Semmeli*. Hard rolls, soft rolls, flaky rolls – what an amazing country! Where else in the world could such a thing happen at six-thirty in the morning?

I bought four or five rolls of each variety from the bakerboy, as he later came to be known in our apartment on the Lake of Zurich. I brought the baked goods into the kitchen, then looked at my watch. It was precisely 6.37. I staggered back to my bed. It was now 6.38, and I had wanted to sleep a bit longer after our strenuous move, hadn't I? I crept between the sheets and dozed off once again, the aroma of those Swiss rolls still in my nostrils.

Then the doorbell rang. Could this be a dream? Of course it was; the bakerboy had entered my subconscious, and I was dreaming about his overflowing basket of Swiss bread and rolls. But the doorbell was still ringing, and whoever was responsible seemed to be growing impatient. I looked at my watch and noted that it was now 6.52.

I felt around the floor again for my slippers and found one of them, which I then put on the wrong foot. My bathrobe was somewhere – now where had I left it? Oh yes, in the kitchen.

I rushed into the kitchen and put on the robe – which was still inside out. The doorbell continued to ring furiously. "I already know that ridiculous story about democracies and dictatorships," I muttered to myself. "It's probably only the milkman…tra-la, tra-la!"

I opened the door with a flourish, and there stood…it couldn't be…the milkman. "Grüezi," I said in my very best and cultivated Swiss-German, which I had perfected the previous day.

"Grüezi, Herr Epstein," came the reply, which puzzled me because there was no way this gentleman could have known me, for we hadn't yet put our name on the door. I must remember, I thought, to ask my wife to take care of this small matter.

The milkman asked what I wished to purchase. He was carrying a metal box filled to the top with milk and cream, yoghurt and butter, cheese and eggs. I looked through his wares carefully and bought five or six of everything. He wrote all this down in a little blue book which he gave me to keep for later payment. Again, I was mightily impressed. What an interesting country! First the bakerboy, then the milkman...and it wasn't even seven o'clock yet. Actually, it was 6.59. I went back to bed and dozed off just as the churchbells were tolling seven o'clock, which they accomplish by ringing twenty-three times. I couldn't quite comprehend why so many separate rings should be necessary to strike the hour of seven, but I had already been through too much that morning to begin questioning the facts of life in Switzerland.

Then the doorbell rang. Oh no! This was a conspiracy, a plain and simple Swiss confederate conspiracy! I knew it. But, for heaven's sake, if they don't want me in their beautiful country, why couldn't they simply say so, instead of going to the trouble of waking me up all the time. I rushed to the door after the usual slipper-and-bathrobe ritual. It was the postman.

"Grüezi," I uttered once again, and the kind man gave me my mail. I asked him why he hadn't put it in the box downstairs and he said that there was no name down there and he wanted to make sure. I made a mental note to ask my wife to put our name on the mailbox as well.

I looked at my watch, the very idea of which was beginning to get on my nerves. As I suspected, it was still too early for such furious activity. It was exactly 7.21.

I went into the living room and turned on the radio. I listened to some excellent Swiss folk music – laendlers and schottisches and so on – and then a voice said, "At the sound of the last tone it will be exactly 7.30." I checked my watch.

Then my wife appeared. She had a sympathetic look on her face as she asked what I was doing up so early. "Early!" I said. You call this early? I've been up since five o'clock, ever since those infernal churchbells started tintinabulating!"

"What churchbells?" she asked.

"Forget it," I said. "But you certainly heard the doorbell ringing, didn't you?"

"I didn't even know we *had* a doorbell," she replied.

"Listen, gorgeous, it rang more than once. It even rang more than twice. To be exact, it rang three times. First there was a boy with bread and rolls, then there was a milkman and then we had the pleasure of a friendly visit from the postman, too."

"What lovely traditions," she said. "Even though I unfortunately didn't hear anything at all. Imagine how nice it will be to live in this country with its milk and rolls and mail! Aren't you glad we moved here?"

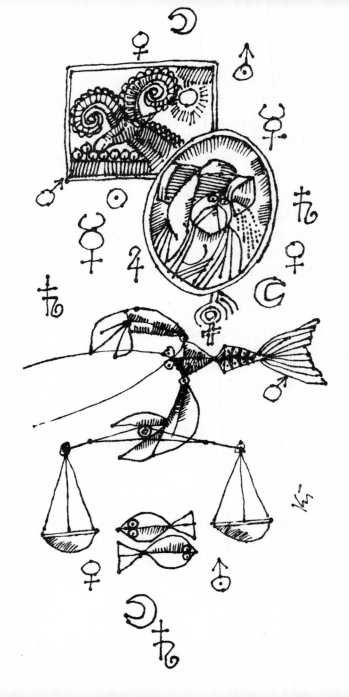

Horrorscope

If you want to be a success in Switzerland – or, for that matter, anywhere in Europe – you must read your horoscope regularly. To the outsider, this might seem to be unimportant, but it's taken quite seriously in Switzerland. For example, it may be all right not to believe in the health-giving qualities of mineral water or mountain air or walking on Sunday, but for heaven's sake you better believe in what the stars are trying to tell you.

To make the whole thing easier for everybody, there are innumerable magazines and newspapers full of this sort of thing. The trouble with the whole business is, just whom do we believe? After all, each astrological analysis appears – on the surface at least – to be different from the others. The only thing they really seem to have in common is that they all deal with the same signs of the zodiac.

My point here is that they're not all really *that* different from each other – it's just that we must make a true and sincere effort to understand the finer, subtler points of what these astrological writers wish to tell us. And, to make the reader's job somewhat easier, I decided some time ago to prepare a single perfect and complete horoscope for everybody in the whole world. It's been a lot of work – a labor of love, one might say. But it was worth it. Now, after all these years, I am pleased to present…my super-duper *All-Time Astrological Astrotable*:

Capricorn, The Goat (22 December–20 January). The Sun and Saturn in your constellation can have an especially good influence on your work and love life. Watch out, though, for petty jealousies and envy on the part of professional colleagues. Try to get along with everyone, even if it seems difficult at first. Remember, Venus knows that you will eventually win your point. As far as health is concerned, avoid late hours and similar excesses. And, if you feel tired in the morning, try to sleep longer or go to bed earlier. It can pay off in the end.

Aquarius, the Water Bearer (21 January–18 February). Everything seems to have crystallized lately. Love, family, profession, health – especially for February Aquariuses – stand under the sign of Pluto the Dog. The star system has crossed the universal plane, and while the Sun may momentarily mess up the magnetic pull of Jupiter, there's really nothing to worry about. You should learn to be more tolerant with officials. After all, they only have your best interests at heart. Flirtations can be fun, too, but bear in mind – especially if you are a January-born Water Bearer – that even the most innocent flirt can sometimes lead further.

Pisces, the Fishes (19 February–20 March). The twentieth century is considered to be most favorable for all Fishes. However, Neptune and Uranus will exert a specific and favorable influence over March-born Fishes after November 23, 1984. The message should therefore be quite clear: watch out for 1984 – but otherwise you certainly have no serious worries. Financially, you could do somewhat better. But patience, industry, tolerance, tact and understanding should eventually bring luck to you in money matters, too. If they don't, try borrowing some Swiss francs at a low interest rate – there are lots of banks in Switzerland. If there is not enough rhythm and harmony in your life, why don't you become a world-famous musician?

Aries, the Ram (21 March–20 April). There's an old proverb which says, "If you can't fight them, Ram it down their throats!" This is where the Ram is fortunate, largely because of the unusual combination afforded by Saturn and Mars. Be sure to conserve your energy – you will need it for civil courage and still bigger things.

Taurus, the Bull (21 April–20 May). Don't get excited over small things. Pettiness is boring and we must all learn to think big and be generous. This is especially important in Switzerland, where a man is recognized for his generosity. However, April Bulls should avoid throwing too many parties, lest they be thought of as April Bull party-throwers. Your love constellation has been favorably influenced by Venus. Your best partner would be an August-born Virgo, the Virgin.

Gemini, the Twins (21 May–21 June). Mercury will probably give you some fancy ideas this month, although you shouldn't count on this. After all, there is no substitute for work, and it would be awful to wait around for some old planet to help you out of a difficult situation. By the way, don't eat too much, either, except for cheese *fondue*. Switzerland produces a lot of cheese and we should all help to eat it up.

Cancer, the Crab (22 June–22 July). I would personally hate to be known as a Cancer or – for that matter – a Crab. According to the latest available statistics, approximately one-twelfth of all people born are Cancers, while nearly fifty per cent are Crabby. But Mars will help you surmount your difficulties. Have faith in Mars,

which, let us remind you, rhymes with "stars".
This should be clear enough.

Leo, the Lion (23 July–23 August). You have a
tendency to disagree with people. This, plus the
interplanetary rambling of Neptune and Venus,
could lead to disagreement with more people.
Either start agreeing or stop talking. Lions are
known for their ferocious approach to most
problems. This is because of the constellation
Neptune-Schneptune. Love looks good.

Virgo, the Virgin (24 August–23 September). Well,
we're not going to bore you today with more
of those old jokes about Virgins. Since there
are no new jokes, we'll have to talk about other
aspects of your astrological problems. You may
have a romance of short duration this month,
but this could depend on many things and possibly might not take place at all. Be sure to write
a letter to an old friend. Try to eat more cheese.
Love looks better all the time.

Libra, the Balance (24 September–23 October).
Everything hangs in the Balance this month.
Have you thought of taking a trip? If you cannot
afford one, take a walk, even a short one. Air is
good, as is Swiss mineral water. Try to be more
tolerant with officials – they need your help. If

you are a female Libra, young, beautiful and with a certain amount of money in the bank, someone might have marriage plans involving you. Love looks great – especially at night.

Scorpio, the Scorpion (24 October–22 November). Don't get involved this month with Rams, Twins or Virgins. Neptune will influence you strongly, but much depends on your own expectations. This might be a good time to tell your boss how much you respect him despite past differences. If he doesn't raise your salary immediately, be patient and understanding.

Sagittarius, the Archer (23 November–21 December). A very important time for Archers. Especially interesting during the first half of December for all Swiss Archers named William Tell. But every apple has its worm. Eat cheese and be kind to officials. Everyone needs love.

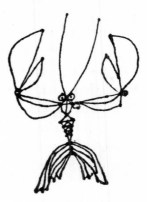

Inside Europe's Insides

The following chapter on Switzerland was prepared for my forthcoming bestseller, "Inside Europe's Insides", or "How to Tell a Fast Franc from a Easy Mark". This important travel guide, produced together with my experienced team of ghostwriters, again opens up the secret door of the "real" Europe to countless numbers of readers the world over. In it, such questions as "What do I do when I've done everything else?" are answered. The chapter on Switzerland offers readers special and exclusive information on how to get the most out of this darling little country nestled among the fabled Alps:

"Inside" Advice for Tourists Arriving in Switzerland. If you are planning to travel to Switzerland by train, be sure to get off your train on time. Switzerland is a relatively small country, and some tourists have been known to end up all over Austria and France without realizing it. One of the best methods to make certain is to ask the friendly conductor to wake you up ten minutes before you reach the Swiss border. A word of advice for our American friends: there is no train service as yet between Europe and the United States, hence the best way to travel to Europe is still by plane or ship.

"Inside" Tips on What to Eat in Switzerland.
Don't do what all the tourists do. Try something new and different, something daring and exciting. For example, there's nothing like a good, old-fashioned Swiss cheese *fondue* to start off or end the day in an unusual way. Cheese *fondue* is one of Switzerland's secret dishes which the editors of "Inside Europe's Insides" can recommend heartily. We've tried one or two varieties ourselves and they really were quite cheesy. Another "inside" Swiss dish is *bratwurst* with *rösti*. *Bratwurst* is a wonderful veal sausage – very long and very white – which is grilled and served with super-delicious *rösti* fried potatoes. Remember, both *fondue* and *bratwurst* are exclusive recommendations of your "Inside Europe's Insides" editors.

What to Buy in Switzerland. Every tourist likes a bargain, and there is every reason to suggest some good ones in Switzerland. However, we definitely advise *against* buying cuckoo clocks. We have learned that Swiss cuckoos *(Cuculus helveticus)* often develop annoying sore throats or laryngitis when they are subjected to the altitude change between Lucerne and New York City. So much for cuckoo clocks. But one unusual suggestion would be to consider buying a Swiss watch. For some time now – the exact number of years escapes us – the Swiss have been manufacturing some very fine and accurate timepieces. But don't take our word for it – go look for yourselves. If you wander around a bit in any Swiss city, you'll probably find a watch store or two.

Now, how about some Swiss cheese, some lace or some chocolate? Here are three products the Swiss can be proud of. So, when in Switzerland, think of something truly unusual to bring back, and remember that you got the idea from the pages of "Inside Europe's Insides". Another "inside" exclusive: there is nothing more typical of Switzerland than a Swiss cow. More and more tourists are considering the possibility of bringing genuine Swiss cows home with them. These Bernese bovines make wonderful gifts, and they're terribly friendly, too. So if you have room in your house or garage, think over this cow idea and surprise your family as they've never been surprised before. Imagine being able to make your own cheese at any hour of the day or night! Or if you simply want some unobtrusive company, turn to everybody's true friend, the cow.

"Inside" Swiss Hotels. Switzerland is full of good hotels. Despite this well-known fact, visitors must nevertheless be careful in making their

overnight arrangements. For example, almost every hotel room in the country is different from the next. Thus décor and quality of the art reproduction over the bed can affect sensitive and discerning travellers. And, speaking of beds, it is most important to mention the number of beds required when ordering a room in Switzerland, for there are rooms with one bed (single rooms) and rooms with two beds (double rooms). There are even rooms with three and more beds, and so on. Also important in the final choice of hotel is the name of the place. Imagine asking a taxi driver to take you to the Hotel Strudelschnecke! This can become quite expensive, too, for by the time you've pronounced the name correctly, the taxi meter will have ticked off an amount of fourteen francs and thirty centimes. Our *exclusive* advice: 1) State the number of beds you wish to have in your room; 2) Specify to the hotel manager whether you want a Van Gogh, a picture of Heidi or the Matterhorn over your bed; 3) Avoid all hotels named Strudelschnecke.

"Inside" Thoughts on What to Do in Switzerland. There are so many things going on in Switzerland that it is difficult to make individual suggestions. But we do suggest that you listen to some fine Swiss yodelling. Yodelling is rather

uncommon in Switzerland these days, what with most yodellers entertaining in Las Vegas, Miami Beach and Budapest. But if you look hard, you're sure to find a cheerful Swiss chalet-type restaurant somewhere or other which features everything from alphorn-blowing to rather ornate yodel technique. The point is: look for it – it's really worth the effort. If you have any difficulty, be sure to ask the desk clerk at your hotel. And be sure to mention that you got the idea from reading "Inside Europe's Insides".

A little bit more esoteric for those of you whose tastes run on a higher plane is an old-fashioned Swiss folk dance festival, which might also include some yodelling if you're lucky. Here, charming Swiss maidens dress up in their native costumes and dance laendlers for the tourists. It's all a lot of fun and worth the trouble. Your hotel desk clerk can give you further details, but we suggest you tell him where you got the idea.

That's it, tourists of the world! Now you're on your own in Switzerland, fabled country nestled among the darling Alps. Have fun in this wonderful place – now that you know it so well. If you discover anything during your visit which has not been mentioned in this chapter, the editors of "Inside Europe's Insides" will be happy to hear from you. In the meantime, as we say in Switzerland, "Ciao, everybody!"

Goodbye, Dolly!

Curling is a rather old game – having originated somewhere or other in the fifteenth century – and there are naturally a lot of old jokes about the sport. Old jokes are all right in their place, but they simply do not blend well with curling, which is a fine and difficult pursuit. To take the wind out of everyone's sails right at the start, I must state that curling simply isn't the old man's game it is thought by many to be.

"Then it's an old lady's game," said my friend Hermann, who had just been named president of the Swiss Anti-Curler's Klub (SACK).

I assured Hermann that I was closer to adolescence than to senility, and that I liked the game very much.

"You like the game," Hermann replied, "because you don't have to wear skis on your feet to participate, and, furthermore, it's a heck of a lot easier than skiing."

"I don't travel into the mountains every winter to wear myself out," I told him. "I like the free and easy camaraderie of the curling clan. They are true sportsmen. Curling requires intense concentration; there is no ranting and raving and rushing about up and down the mountains. This is the difference, *old* man, although I'm still not sure you understand me."

"Well, to tell you the truth, I don't...and I don't think I want to!" Hermann said.

"Then let me explain it to you. Imagine standing on the smoothest, most perfect piece of ice in the world – a shiny battlefield in the crisp, health-giving air of the Alps."

"Go on, old fellow," Hermann interjected.

"Well," I continued, "there you are, wanting to learn something about the distinguished sport of curling, just as I was last year at this time. And look at me today: a master curler already! Anyway, the first thing you notice is that somebody offers you some stones with handles on them. These are what our irreverent friends call hot-water bottles. But they're fine stones – heavy, polished granite from the Scottish quarries at Mauchline in Ayershire or Ailsa Craig in the Firth of Clyde."

"Firth things firth, please," said Hermann. "Or should I simply take you for granite?"

"Hermann," I countered, "I just finished talking about old jokes. For your information – once and for all – I know *every* curling joke you can think of. So be quiet, and learn something for a change!" I then continued my lesson:

"Curling is played on a rink by a rink. That is to say, there is a rink which is a number of yards long and then there are the teams, which are also called rinks. There are circles – called 'houses' –

at both ends of the rinks, the ice rinks, I mean, not the people rinks. The circles contain a number of additional concentric circles to help scoring, although the individual circles have absolutely nothing to do with the number of points one gets. The center of the house is called the tee, and on the tee there stands a 'dolly', which is like a bowling pin. The dolly is extremely important, but it can be removed anytime by the skip, who is the captain."

"If dolly is so important," asked Hermann, "why can she be removed by the captain, or would you rather *skip* that question?"

"Dolly is a thing, not a she; and stop your infernal punning! It must be terrible living with you. How in heaven's name can your wife stand all those horrible plays on words? Now, let's get on with our curling – I think you'll learn to like it after a time.

"The dolly, as I said, is extremely important, although, quite frankly, she – I mean, *it* – has virtually nothing to do with the game, other than serving as – well – a focal point of everything that's happening on the ice – I mean, the rink. Now, to continue, each team, consisting of four players each, shoots eight stones into the opposing house. The players are directed by their own skip who tells them to curl in or curl out. Curling is the name of the game and it comes from the fact that the stones are not bowled down the ice, but are 'curled' down, with an 'in' curl or an 'out' curl. The stones are then able to describe various curves so that they avoid other stones – and so on.

"Now, one of the most important things to know about this marvellous game is that you can't play it without a broom in one hand."

"Now that's a sweeping statement," said Hermann. "Continue, I'm bristling with excitement!"

"The purpose of the broom is to sweep the ice in front of the stones, but only when the skip says so. For example, if your skip wants a particular curve on the stone, he allows it to reach a certain point on the ice and then calls for the other two members of your team to sweep in front of it. This melts the ice a bit and prevents the curling stone from continuing its curve. The stone changes direction and ostensibly ends up where the skip wanted it to in the first place. I forgot to mention from the very beginning that the skip stands at the other end of the ice and gives directions – using *his* broom to point to the spot where he wants the various stones to end up. There are a lot of other details, of course, but basically the idea is for one team to get as many of their stones as close to the middle as possible without having an opposing stone between them. I mean, one stone near the tee or dolly counts one point, the next stone another point, but only one team can make points. Is that clear?"

"No, but with you nothing ever is."

"Now, when all sixteen stones – each, incidentally, weighing around 44 pounds – have been shot, then that is called the end."

"Thank heavens!" cried Hermann.

"No, not the end of the game. Just the *first* end. Each game consists of nine or eleven or thirteen ends, depending on how the players feel. Then the whole thing starts all over again, but in the opposite direction. Fun, don't you think?"

"No, not especially. And, anyway, I don't like sweeping – I get enough of it at home. But I sure like to sweep late in the morning, that I can tell you!"

"As I was saying," I continued, "the most important thing about the game is that the skip is always right. If he places his broom on a particular spot and says 'play it,' you play it. He's the boss. In other words, he stands at the top of the rink and points with his broom."

"Oh, you mean like 'broom at the top'!"

"Yes, exactly. That broom you treat so lightly, sir, is the scepter of the curler. No honorable curler would ever be seen without one. Now, for your information, here are some other details: learn where the 'hog' is, watch out for the 'sweeping score' and always remember the difference between the normal side and keen side of your stone. Sweep when the skip tells you and stop when he says 'up' and make sure you play the stones with the right color bubbles. If you give an 'in handle' when you're told to and an 'out' when it's asked for, you'll have absolutely no trouble with the bubble. Keep your foot on the crampit or in the hack and, whatever you do, play the broom. Now, do you think you understand a bit more?"

"I suppose so, except for one thing."

"What's that, Hermann?"

"Are you off your dolly?"

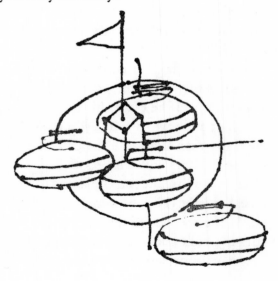

Ye Olde Yodel

On August 1, 1991, Switzerland will celebrate its seven-hundredth anniversary as a confederation. As this important occasion approaches, it might be fitting to consider some of the factors which have contributed to this unusual record among modern-day countries.

One need not be an expert in Swiss history to understand why the Swiss are so successful at keeping their country in one recognizable piece. After all, there are not many nations these days which manage to exist for more than a century or two. What, then, is Switzerland's secret? This question fascinated me as well, and I immediately arranged to hire fourteen assistants from the local Society of Writers (SOW) to help me undertake what would soon become a major research project.

After thirty-three months of intensive study, our research group appears to have arrived at a number of valid conclusions which could, if viewed in the proper light, lend credence to those forces which are frequently at play in a nation as complicated and diverse as Switzerland is reputed to be. In other words, we're not entirely sure what we're doing. But we do have some random thoughts on this complex and diverse little country and we shall present them at the next United Readers' International Convention (URIC) to be held in Mitlödi, Canton of Glarus, in May 1984.

Without anticipating the results of our study, one can nevertheless assume that there are many factors which have most definitely contributed to Switzerland's success as a serious nation over the past centuries. The first factor is that Switzerland has virtually no natural resources – excluding, of course, the Swiss-German language. This means that there are simply no resources to use up, and thus no serious worry. As a result, Switzerland was forced to invent some resources. One of these was the Yodel.

The Yodel

Switzerland developed and patented the standard form of yodel long before the people of other countries ever thought of standing on mountaintops and screeching at the top of their lungs. The reasons for this development are manifold. Most important is the fact that Switzerland has always had numerous mountaintops. This means that half the battle was won before the yodel itself was invented. Another point in Switzerland's favor was that they really didn't believe in war as a practical solution to man's problems – and the Swiss have always been extremely practical. Of course, there had always

been minor battles in Switzerland – disagreements with one's neighbors and so on – just as there are today. But the result of having no wars meant that Switzerland's male population was not decimated, as were those of other, supposedly more powerful, countries. With so many males hanging around, Switzerland had to find an intelligent use for them, mainly because there were few well-paying jobs in those days.

So the Swiss cantons got together and decided that all male Swiss citizens would thereafter be subject to mountain duty in the Corps of Relatively Peaceful Service (C.O.R.P.S.), which was the country's equivalent of an army. Every male citizen between the ages of forty-one and forty-three was obliged to serve guard duty on a mountain peak no further than sixteen kilometers from his own home. Each Swiss male then had to learn a secret and cryptic method of communicating with his neighbor on the next peak. This was the earliest form of yodelling and was only used when there was imminent danger of attack. In the early days of the Confederation, one could often hear messages being yodelled from one Alp to another by the shimmering light of the silvery moon. Later, as the country grew more independent and secure, the yodelling stopped. Today, there is relatively little yodelling in Switzerland, even when the moon shines.

The few surviving exponents of modern Swiss yodelling can be found today in countries as far away as Germany and Austria, where they entertain diners in modern Swiss chalet-type restaurants designed to acquaint foreigners with the hidden strengths and moral fiber of the valiant Swiss people.

The Chalet

When the Swiss Confederation was formed, there were great differences among the Helvetians on just what should constitute a dwelling-place. Older members of the population insisted on tents. Others wanted to establish the Habsburg-type castle as a standard for everyone. This problem created great tension, dissension and attention in Switzerland until a young fellow named Walti, who lived in a small hamlet called Hohle Gasse (Hollow Alley), hit upon a new and revolutionary idea.

"I have a new and revolutionary idea," he told his fellow townsmen of Hohle Gasse.

The townsmen replied in chorus: "Revolutionary ideas are as bad as communism." Of course, modern communism hadn't yet been invented, but in those days communism meant the tradition of serving herring in tomato sauce for Sunday brunch – the so-called red herrings.

In any case, Walti was not discouraged. He had

been studying architecture at the Federal Institute of Technology (FIT) and he proceeded to convince his neighbors of what he had in mind. What he had in mind was a house that would reflect the basic spirit of the country, one which could later be portrayed on travel posters all over the world. And thus the chalet was born.

But there was no one around who could build one, except for one of Walti's neighbors from Hohle Gasse. His name was Willibald H. Tell, who had just been awarded an honorary doctorate from the University of Canton bearing the inscription, "For saving your little country in time of great peril." Dr. Tell was actually a carpenter who specialized in building bigger and better crossbows. Walti thought that Tell could probably help in the design and construction of the world's first chalet.

But Dr. Tell was nowhere to be found. When Walti looked for him in his modest hut in Hohle Gasse, he found no one at home, not even Tell's butler, Gessler. Walti asked around a bit and learned that Tell had departed on a lecture tour sponsored by the West Orange Apple Growers Association (WOAGA). So Walti went elsewhere in his search for advice.

He went to Sweden. There he managed to interest a group of financiers in building prefabricated parts for Swiss chalets. He also founded the first export business for prefabricated Swiss restaurants, and he sent complete buildings all over the world to spread the idea of fine Swiss living everywhere. Today we all know what a Swiss chalet looks like, even though – with today's prices – most people will never be able to afford one. As so few people realize the deeper significance of the chalet, one should take time to have dinner in a genuine Swiss chalet restaurant – whether it be in New York, Amsterdam or Melbourne. Then bear in mind, as you sit in those hallowed surroundings eating your *fondue* amid the cowbells and authentic yodel music, that you are indirectly paying homage to the stalwart Swiss who established the Confoederatio Helvetica almost seven hundred years ago.

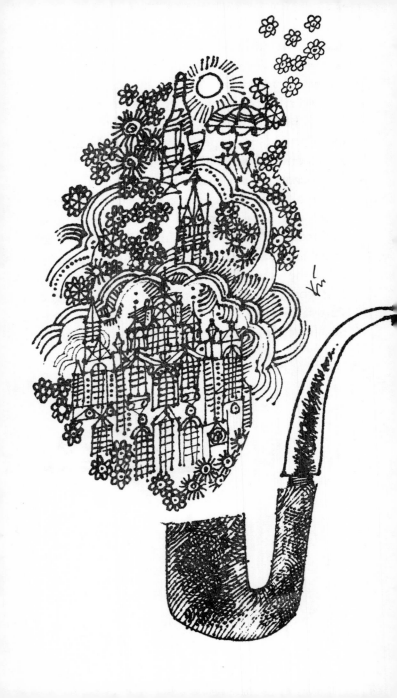

Pipe Dreams

The art of pipe-smoking was developed many years ago by the British, who even then tried to do everything possible – short of central heating – to keep themselves warm. Now that Britain has joined the Common Market, the country is exporting pipes by the thousands, and everyone – the Germans, the French, the Swiss – has suddenly discovered that pipe-smoking is considerably more challenging for the mind than the old system of puffing away at anything combustible and smoke-producing.

I used to laugh at the mystique of pipe-smoking. After all, how could it possibly matter if you break in a pipe or not? And what was all this nonsense about tobacco – the types, the cuts, the aromas? So I decided to buy myself a few pipes and try. The first thing I learned is that I would have to take a three-month course in pipology given at Stem University in Asheville. This is in Old Smoky country, and I was happy to visit the area again after so many years.

It is quite clear to me that few of my readers will be able to attend such a course, so I have decided to provide a condensed version of what I learned there. The only problem is that I'm still a bit confused myself, but you should get the general idea anyway. Because once you've learned how to smoke a pipe correctly – which takes no more than twenty years – you can really start to live as you've never lived before.

Obviously, the first thing is to buy some pipes – and here the material, the form, the weight and the grain play an extremely important role. As far as shapes are concerned, I prefer Tomatoes to Bulldogs, and Bulldogs to Churchwardens, and I think most people would agree. It is also good to think about the wood, which is usually bruyère grown in France – very close to the Swiss border – and originally discovered by the British. Once you've purchased your first pipe, you will be ready to join the international fraternity of those who prefer a polished piece of old briar to anything in this world, including a nonsmoking girl friend.

The next thing to do is to talk to someone who knows a great deal about the art and aesthetics of pipe-smoking, because nothing is of greater value than someone else's experience. This is what I did when I visited my friend Walti.

"Hi, Walti," I murmured as I entered my friend's office in Zurich. "Are you there, old boy?" "Yes, here I am, Eugene – behind that great cloud of smoke to the left of where you're standing. No...not there!...Here, yeah, that's it."

I finally saw Walti through the haze and somehow managed to find and shake his hand. "Hi, Walti," I repeated, "how are you and that little stinkpot pipe of yours this morning?"

"Listen, chum," Walti replied. "I see no reason for you to be so aggressive at this time of the morning, nor do I understand – to be frank – why you insist on shaking my left foot instead of my right hand."

I was amazed myself. "Your foot? Sorry, old boy, it was only a question of visibility, not to mention what's happening to my lungs, which were built, I might add, for the respiration of oxygen. I'm sorry if I shook your foot – I really am, especially since I don't recall your hands being so calloused. But anyway, old friend, I came here to learn something about the fine art of smoking a pipe."

And so Walti, after some protest, decided to accept me as his student – and this was even before I attended Stem University in Asheville.

"Now what you've got to do," he told me, "is to use the reamer in the bowl and the cleaner in the stem. Make sure you get a snap-proof peg and insist on vulcanite. Smoke your pipe cool and tamp it down carefully. Breaking-in means carbonizing the bowl, evenly and over a period of several months."

"What is this – a joke?" I asked.

"Yes, it's a joke," said Walti. "And if you'd like

to hear some more witticisms, why don't you kindly ask me to continue?"

"Please, do by all means continue," I muttered sheepishly.

"There are many different kinds of pipes and many different kinds of tobacco," Walti said. "There are many different brands, many different tools and accessories, and many different stems. There are many different prices and many different smells..."

"Most of them awful!" I interjected.

"Especially when *you're* in the room," Walti added.

"Touché, friend," I replied. "When it comes to rejoinders, you're the best comedian in the world. But please proceed with your lecture on how to foul up the atmosphere."

"The first thing to remember," my mentor told me, "is to learn what it is you like to smoke and what kind of cut you prefer. The fine-cut tobaccos burn hot but you don't have to keep relighting them. I prefer Cavendish to Curly Cut with an occasional bit of Granulated – although this is completely optional and personal. The main thing is to buy no more than forty or fifty different kinds of tobacco and find out which one leaves you the least nauseous after you smoke it. If you get that far, it's just like taking immunizations against hay fever."

"Hey!" I suggested, "what about smoking hay – the way we used to when we were kids?"

"I haven't noticed that you are not a kid today," Walti replied.

"Touché again, old fellow. What do we do next?"

"I was talking about tobaccos, remember?" said friend Walti. "Now for heaven's sake let me finish a sentence! There is Virginia tobacco and there's Maryland and Shag and English and Oriental Ready-Rubbed and Flake. And in each category there are five or six hundred different choices and, of course, an infinite number of mixture possibilities. Now, once you've decided how many dozen different tobaccos you wish to try, and after you've spoken to your banker about arranging the suitable credit, you must get some pipes, preferably a few Dunhills, mainly because anyone who is anyone smokes a Dunhill, which has a little white dot on the stem to distinguish it from other brands."

"They do sound great," I said, "even if they *wouldn't* have a little dot on the stem."

"And then," Walti continued, "don't forget a tobacco jar, a reamer, a scraper, some cleaners, a number of pipe stands, a carbon cutter and a carrying case or two. If you want to economize, you can buy forty instead of fifty pipes and you can always start with a small collection of tobaccos. And be sure to fill the bowls only at the bottom when you're breaking them in...except in the case of Meerschaums...and be sure to clean them well...and let them rest for forty-two hours every day...and be sure to insure them... and be sure..."

I had to interrupt him. "Walti," I groaned impatiently. "I still prefer girls."

The Simple Life

When I was a boy on Long Island there was no such thing as a supermarket. As a result, everything we bought usually came from a small specialty store. How well I remember my mother carefully choosing the live chicken which would soon – alas for it! – end up on our Sunday dinner table. And some of my earliest memories of the world of commerce concern a small delicatessen store in a remote Long Island village. I no longer remember precisely where the store was located, because everything in that area has now become one long monotonous row of undulating traffic and sprawling suburbia.

That particular delicatessen – wherever it was – holds memories for me which I would have some trouble explaining to my psychiatrist – even if I had one. That store – that simple, straightforward store – seems today to symbolize the uncomplicated life I think we must have led at that time. Perhaps I was pampered and perhaps I was sheltered by my parents from the evils of the grown-up world, but, for some reason, that life – especially on Long Island – was uncomplicated and full of delicatessens and bakeries and butcher-shops and places that sold live chickens for the Sunday dinner table.

This particular delicatessen, as I started to say,

remains in my memory because it was there that we used to buy butter and flour and pickles out of open containers. The butter – rich and yellow and awfully buttery-looking – was kept in a smooth wooden tub and was sold in chunks and by weight. I recall how the delicatessen man used to cut out chunks of butter with a menacingly large knife – and then he would weigh them and wrap them in wax paper. And roughly the same thing happened with his pickles and with his flour and, if I'm not mistaken, with his coffee, because the roasted beans were also kept in large barrels and sold by weight in lined paper bags.

As everyone knows by this time, the small specialty shops in America began disappearing as the new, more efficient self-service markets gradually gained acceptance. This was many years before the same thing began happening in Europe, and now, of course, it's happening here too.

What fascinates me about the whole business is that I've been through it twice, which leaves me with an odd and almost mysterious feeling of *déjà vu*. For when I first came to Switzerland more than two decades ago, I was fascinated by the fact that the same type of store I knew from my childhood was apparently quite common in Switzerland. I saw no tubs of butter, but I don't remember looking for them either. But there were tiny grocery stores run by tiny old ladies who sold everything imaginable in an area no larger than a hall closet. And then there were those marvellous Swiss bakeries with little windows which opened onto the street, where strangers like myself could buy *pâtisserie* and drip jelly and powdered sugar all over their clothes on the way home.

I learned a great deal about Switzerland from those little stores. The tiny old ladies were invariably polite and helpful. They never failed to say "Grüezi", nor did they hesitate to help me with my impossibly confused German. They even worried about me if I didn't appear for my daily liter of milk. "Were you ill yesterday, Herr Epstein?" they used to ask – not just to make conversation, but because they were genuinely interested in my welfare. Such treatment was quite normal in Switzerland, just as it must have been on Long Island some years earlier.

My purpose here is not to lament the passing of the small specialty shop, because I would feel rather idiotic to stand in the way of progress – even if it would help. I happen to enjoy supermarkets. I think they are most efficient, and I'm sure that – dollar for dollar or franc for franc – we're all possibly better off in the end. But I'm not quite so sure what technology and efficiency and data processing will leave us with once the human element has been even more efficiently eliminated.

I even wonder sometimes whether recapturing thoughts of butter sold in open tubs is such a noble thing. It happens to cross my mind from time to time, and there's not much I can do about it. And it's not only the butter – it was the period itself.

The tobacco stores somewhere in the old city of Zurich still exist, as do the bakeries. The red-faced old butcher still hacks away at pigs' feet with his cleaver, and there are still a few grocers who haven't yet given up, haven't yet disappeared forever. And, with some luck, there will always be a few fine old people who will continue to operate their stores as they have in the past. And perhaps they will operate them long enough so that the next generation can nostalgically look back – as I am doing right now – and reminisce about their little delicatessen store – somewhere, sometime, run by somebody, where butter used to be sold out of open wooden tubs.

About Trout

I've always admired fishing as a sport, and I feel comfortable in the company of genuine piscatorial experts. There is something peaceful and reassuring about such people, for they refuse to be caught up in the hectic ways and general madness of everyday life. On the other hand, I doubt that fish very much care for fishermen – experts or otherwise – for a fish's life would be less hectic were it not for the barbed hook. By the same token, so would a worm's life.

Actually, it's not entirely fair to catch fish. Some varieties are rather stupid and generally take the bait, allowing themselves to be hauled up without a fight or even a faint wriggle. Other varieties are smarter than we are – which doesn't mean too much – and rarely allow themselves to be taken without a devil of a fight. Such a fish is the trout.

One thing about the trout family is that hardly a member would dream of living in polluted water for very long. Either they seek cleaner, more habitable surroundings or they just plain die. This is rather intelligent if one thinks about it a bit. Human beings – presumably the highest form of animal life – don't mind living in bad air or swimming in sloppy water. The trout expires quickly under such circumstances. We die more

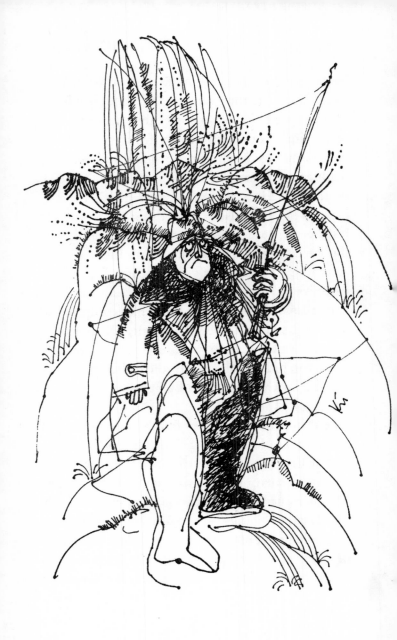

slowly and usually blame it on something else anyway.

Because of his penchant for cleanliness, the trout has unwittingly gotten himself into a stew, both literally and figuratively, for fish who live in clean waters also happen to taste good.

Switzerland is an excellent place for trout fishing. The country has everything one needs to pursue this sport: crystal streams which rush down from the mountains and trout to swim in them. Anyway, this is what my friend Freddy told me when he asked if I would join him for a spot of trout fishing.

I immediately accepted the invitation and could already taste, in my mind's eye, the delicate flavor of *truite au bleu* with melted brown butter.

Freddy suggested I bring along a pair of hip boots so that we could wade in the stream from time to time. He also told me that our stream was off in the back of one Switzerland's most famous mountains – Pilatus, I think it was – and the countryside in that area was beautiful and fascinating and picturesque and romantic.

We left for the back of Pilatus early the following Saturday morning, I with my brand-new Japanese hip boots, Freddy with everything else, including rods, reels, hooks, spinners, leaders, floats, weights, line, a box of cigars and some flypaper. On the way to Pilatus we discussed the strategy of the day. Freddy was obviously quite experienced and he knew the stream well. He told me of the good and bad habits of mountain brook trout and how careful thought and quick action could outwit them in the end. I was eager to arrive at our destination. I felt sure of myself and wanted to show Freddy that my years of catching flounders, eels and blackheads in Long Island Sound had not been entirely wasted.

Soon we arrived in a small village in a quaint section of the country called Entlebuch, which probably means something if anyone would care to check into it. Freddy stopped the car in front of the local inn and suggested we have a cup of tea. When we got inside, a friendly Swiss lady brought us a huge platter of cold meats, another of cheese and a third with rolls, butter, jam und honey. "Grüezi, Freddy!" she said, as she placed this mighty load in front of us. "Off to catch a few trout again?" Freddy replied that we would probably start fishing in an hour or two – as soon as we finished our morning snack. After we had downed our fourth cup of tea and seventh ham-and-cheese sandwich, I suggested we try our luck with the trout. Freddy, who was just lighting one of his favorite morning cigars, gurgled a bit from the gastrointestinal area and nodded affirmatively.

When we arrived at the stream, I was somewhat disappointed. There were lots and lots of rocks, but not much water. So Freddy and I decided to split up – he would walk ahead and fish one side of the stream, I would lag behind and fish the other bank.

"One thing," he said to me. "When you get to that dam up ahead, be sure to climb carefully over it, because it's slippery and I don't want to lose you as I did my other friends."

"Don't you worry, friend," I muttered under my breath, my teeth clenched. "I can take anything you can take. Let's be off!"

Soon I was playfully testing the depth of the various pools of water in the stream. It was a beautiful day, with the sun reflected a million times in the ripples made by my Japanese boots. But there were no trout in sight, for these cunning fish sincerely dislike sunlight.

Then I came to the dam. It didn't seem much to climb – a mere question of pulling myself up and over some wet logs and mossy rocks. It certainly wasn't more than ten or fifteen feet high at the most. But it looked much easier than it turned out to be. In the first place, I was a few ounces heavier than I was the last time I tried to scale a dam, and now I was doing it in my Japanese hip boots with a fishing rod in one hand and the last bite of ham-and-cheese sandwich in the other. But I finally got over without much more to show for the treacherous experience than a skinned elbow and hurt pride. As I came over the top, I noticed that the stream itself had changed greatly. It was no longer a collection of gray rocks and still pools; it was now a rushing, gushing, full-fledged mountain river. I looked far ahead and perceived that it was now flowing through a deep ravine, and that the ravine, which looked more and more ominous to me, was pointed straight up towards Pilatus, from which it emerged. Now I had no choice but to walk in the water, for there were no banks, just cliffs of rock and a jungle of tangled foliage. I proceeded to walk and fish, casting my gleaming spinner right and left as I moved slowly ahead.

Soon I was no longer walking – I was climbing again, first on my normal two legs, then on all fours, with the cool mountain water spashing all over my face. There were waterfalls, cataracts, whirlpools, wildly tossing surf. I had never climbed up a waterfall before, and I found it to be a new and exhilarating experience. I was free; I was a salmon! Then I slipped.

Perhaps the soles of my Japanese boots were not accustomed to the slippery rocks of this Swiss stream. Perhaps I was no longer as agile as I had once been. Whatever the reason, I fell, with a great deal of certitude and little indecision. I smashed into the middle of an icy-clear pool and my knee struck hard rock.

I was soaked through and my leg was numb. I tried to climb further; now the stream resembled a mountaineer's nightmare, with huge wet boulders and tremendous waterfalls. There appeared to be no way out of this watery trap and my knee refused to cooperate further.

I sat down on a flat stone to meditate, for, in moments like this, clear thought and contemplation are of greater value than my normal fear and cowardice. I made up my mind to forge forward until I could find Freddy.

Eventually – after what seemed like decades – I saw Freddy again. Sheer strength and courage had helped me through one of the six great crises of my life. My knee remained stiff for seven weeks, but there was nothing more to show for my experience – no fish, either, except for the two small ones Freddy had caught. "Come on!" he said gleefully. "Let's go back to the restaurant and have them cooked."

"With pleasure," I gasped. "And don't forget the melted brown butter!"

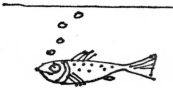

Party Lines

"Aren't you the author of...uh...that funny little book called...?" The lady addressing me was my designated table neighbor at a birthday party we recently attended. Her husband interrupted her impatiently:

"Of course you know who he is. He's that writer fellow, the one who wrote about the Föhn and Fondue and similar jokes."

"That's what I said, he's...the...why good evening, doctor, how are you? Isn't it absolutely lovely here in this old cellar?"

"What a delightful idea those marvellous people had. Oh, you must be the humorous writer. How about telling us a funny story or two?"

"I'm sorry," I murmured in my best Swiss-German, "I really don't speak Swiss-German all that well."

"But he writes all about us – imagine, without speaking Swiss all that well!"

"I don't think that's so interesting."

"I do."

"Tell me, Mr. Epstein, how does it feel to have all that talent?"

"Well, to tell you the truth," I said, "I really don't like to refer to *anybody* as being talented – in fact, I never did. Imagine calling Toscanini 'the talented conductor'."

"But you're not even Italian – ha, ha!" Another female guest had joined our table.

"Say," I said, "you really *are* talented."

"I thought you never used that awful word."

Nuts, I thought. Her motor started again with a plaintive whine.

"Look at that strange man over there. Is that a decoration he's wearing around his neck?" "It must be, someone said so."

"It couldn't be," I said, "because this is supposed to be an informal birthday party for one of my best friends – so it must be a practical joke."

"Well, if that's what it is, it's not very funny."

A general discussion began. "Perhaps he's really an aristocrat...there are some Swiss aristocrats left, you know." "Yeah, but if he's an aristocrat, he doesn't have to go around with an iron cross – or whatever it is – around his neck."

"Then it's a joke."

"He looks degenerate to me. Of course, all aristocrats are basically degenerate."

"What's an aristocrat anyway, especially in Switzerland?"

"That's somebody who either stole or bought a title so long ago that nobody really remembers how or when he got it."

"Tell me, Mr. Epstein, how does it feel to be a writer?"

"I don't know," I replied. "Why don't you ask Ernest Hemingway?"

"Mr. Epstein, how do you get rid of aggressions, anyway?"

"By hitting people over the head."

"That guy is really funny, isn't he, Max?"

"I think we all ought to have a drink."

"I've been drinking all the time."

"Then let's have another…I really don't understand, Mr. Epstein, why you never learned to speak the Swiss-German language."

"Because I can't – I'm too stupid."

"Oh! isn't he amusing!"

"Yes, I really am – I mean, I didn't say that to be amusing. I'm too stupid to learn Swiss-German because I would have to study anthropology and zoology to master all those special sounds so typical of the language."

"I resent that," someone said.

"Resent what? Mr. Epstein's only defending himself against what I consider an absolutely unjustifiable attack on your part."

"Oh, let's dance – let's everybody go and have a nice little dance."

"I don't like to dance."

"I do."

"I do sometimes. My husband likes to dance because of the movement." "I like rhythm."

"I *got* rhythm!"

"I don't like to dance, because I'm really not very good at it…anyway, I always begin to sweat like a water buffalo."

"How crude!"

"Sorry."

"Do you really think that's an Iron Cross?"

"Of course it's not an Iron Cross! He must be Swiss nobility from way back."

"I think he's a fraud."

"Well, if he is, he ain't the only one. What about our writer friend here?"

"You mean," I asked, "you think I'm a fraud? Because if you do, you are quite right – for a change."

"But why does that nobleman over there come dressed like an overstuffed monkey?"

"Come on, dear, leave him alone – we already mentioned that he looks degenerate. He probably doesn't know what he's doing, that's all."

"This wine is awfully good."

"Yes, it is…at least *I* think so."

"I like it, too."

"The food was marvellous."

"Amazing."

"Who wants to dance now?"

"Come on, Max, tell us how it feels to be a famous professor."

"I would rather do what Mr. Epstein does."

"Max, don't be so modest."

"What's the name of that book again...I have it on the tip of..."

"I wouldn't like to be that waitress, with all those things to carry around the place."

"The book is all about Switzerland...with funny stories and all."

"Tell us some, Mr. Epstein...please tell us some funny stories."

"I'm not a comedian – honestly I'm not. In fact, I'm even rather introverted."

"Was ist das?" "Introvertiert." "Ach so!"

"Are you really?"

"No."

"Then why did you say so?"

"Because I'm supposed to be funny. Remember?"

"Isn't he terribly amusing, Max? I told you you'd like him."

"Who said I liked him?"

"I like me," I suggested.

"There he goes again."

"There's one other thing about this party I thought I should add. Our host and hostess are about the finest, most generous, dearest friends one could ever want..."

"Yes." "Absolutely." "Simply grand."

"I mean it!"

"Are you being funny again?"

"No, and if I were, Paul would understand."

"Who's Paul?"

"A saint – ho, ho, ho!"

"But what about that fellow with the medal on his chest; he never even dances with anyone."

"Thank God!"

"I thought they didn't give medals in Switzerland."

"They don't. Only during the Olympics."

"When were the Olympic games last held in Switzerland – and where? Does anybody know?"

"St. Moritz…1947?"

"I thought it was 1948."

Rallye Round the Spitfive, Girls!

In olden days, especially in springtime, a young man's fancy used to turn to thoughts of love. This was plain and simple fact, and everybody knew it. There is no less love today, but it appears to be of a different variety. "It's darned nice to have a girl friend," we overheard one young gentleman saying recently, "but what good is a girl if you haven't got a car?"

Ironically enough, it is also in spring that our fancy turns to thoughts of automobiles. This is no coincidence, either. For in the spring, we young males – all of us who can get away with it – don our plumage in the form of shiny paint and gleaming chrome and set out in quest of whatever nature has in store for us.

It simply does not befit the male of the species to droop around the place in dull browns and grays. Look at the ducks. Look at the rest of the animal kingdom. We are the mallards of the genus *homo sapiens*, but instead of flying and croaking "quack-quack", we drive wildly about the neighborhood, disturbing the peace with our "honk-honks". Perhaps a comparison with geese might have been more apt.

I do not subscribe to the theory that the current automobile madness is a sublimated continuation of childhood, and that all we're really doing is playing, just as our children play with their miniature cars. No, and I must repeat this: the automobile urge is strongest in the springtime, and don't forget it. That's my theory, and it's the result of lots of study, most of it based on my own observations.

The trouble with cars is that the kind we'd really like to have are generally rather expensive. The mallard can sport his plumage at no immediate cost to himself. This is because the animal kingdom is backward, and there's not an animal anywhere in this world – with the exception of man – who has learned to appreciate the benefits of good old hard cash. So, anyway, the mallard can show off for nothing – including the built-in horn – and he probably attains his personal goal more often than his human counterparts. There are, however, few surveys available to prove this last assumption.

We know that automobiles are expensive. We also know that many automobiles are relatively inexpensive – only *some* are really expensive. Then why is it that we crave the more expensive ones? I know the answer to that question, too: because we want to be different from the next fellow. After all, anybody can purchase a cheap car, but there are few of us who can afford an *Albee-Rodeo Super-12 Spitfive!* In fact, since I can't anyway, that leaves only two such dream cars in all of Switzerland, one red, the other yellow (with lavender racing stripes).

Now what's so special about special cars (forgetting the price, of course)? Let's discuss the Albee-Rodeo Super-12 Spitfive. This is what it offers:

Chassis

Super spot-welded 4-mm hot-spun extruded steel throughout, with a modicum of nickel-plated gum alloy in all trouble areas, including an undercoating of spearmint, corrosion-resistant and rust-free. Twenty-four nugents protect the driver and his passenger from undue shock, while cracklocks assure a trouble-free and rattle-free undercarriage. Available in 14 and 18 carats, with 12-cm undulating spread.

Engine

Nine cylinders, each 3.2673 liters, direct firing line and squad, dual-injection twin carburetors, super-start air-oil-water-petrol-gasoline mixture. Double camshaft, self-lubricating windscreen washer, sealed head and feet, 14-inch eccentric off-center beaming rods, thremthrow silversteel stainless bearings throughout, 23.5-inch push, 6.3-inch pull, 19-inch throw under normal operating conditions.

Interior

Ebony GT (Go-Tee) instrument panel and fittings, hand-fashioned in Tahiti. Innumerable instruments, including tachometer, schwarzometer and eatermeter. Eight-step intruding, floor-mounted sports shift stick with ivory handle hand-carved in Bulgaria. Four-stage stereo horn, adjustable from pianissimo to fortississimo, which plays first five notes of Japanese national anthem (provided as an optional extra on most models). Seats are reclining, sliding, leaning type with dielectric constant control within easy reach. Bamboo and bean-sprout steering wheel destroys itself, for added safety, upon slightest exterior impact. Realistic holes on metal spokes of steering wheel create a racy feeling which is carried through the entire elegant interior of all models. Velvet upholstery, with Rhodesian tufting and special smashing, handspun and tufted in Columbus, Ohio. *Safety features:* platinum ignition key to turn off the engine under emergency conditions: Radio transmitter which automatically sends an SOS signal to the next police station if car is stolen or turns over: Built-in Okinawan silk parachute for more effective braking at high speeds.

144

Miscellaneous

The Albee-Rodeo Super-12 Spitfive has ample room in its splendid luggage compartment for 4320 cubic inches of baggage, placed either obversely, conversely or simply versely. (This is the equivalent of one small suitcase.) The engine compartment contains various items of equipment – chiefly the engine – with a special area near the fuel injection pump for one repair kit containing a screwdriver, a hammer and a pair of pliers. Special wheel discs give wheels the appearance of turning when they are stopped and of being stopped when they are turning. The Albee-Rodeo Super-12 Spitfive has been generously designed to accommodate two persons: the driver and his female companion.

Body & Finish

Albee-Rodeo models 12-a, 12-b and B-52 have bodies designed and built by Giacomo Puccetti at the Carrosseria Prosciutto plant near Parma. They are deliverable in forty-five different colors, either mixed together or in various combinations which can be discussed with any Albee representative.

General

The Albee-Rodeo Super-12 Spitfive offers the discerning racing enthusiast all the pleasures of driving, without the displeasures of feeling inferior, unimportant and downright stupid. An Albee-Rodeo Spitfive driver is an Albee-Rodeo Spitfive driver, and it hardly matters which of the sixteen basic models he chooses – the less expensive ($72,000) Royal Double-Dip or the mighty and incomparably magnificent ($129,560, fully equipped) Astor Cougats-Tigerrag.

Jet Pet

Society is society the world over, and Switzerland is no exception. Yet there is little pretentiousness among the Swiss, who are known as pragmatic and down-to-earth. As a result, the height of high society is a bit lower than in most other parts of the world, for the Swiss have virtually everything they want – and thus considerably less reason to display their snobbery on their sleeves. One or two examples may serve to make this point clear:

In New York, it is considered "in" to speak French at a garden party. In France, it is considered "in" to speak English at a garden party. In England, it is considered "in" to speak American at a garden party. Where does this leave us?

In Switzerland, one can speak any language at all – with no fear that anybody will even notice. This means that language is not the "in" thing with the Swiss, but just a sorry old means of communication, which it was supposed to be in the first place. But what about that insidious little word "in"?

A lot of people enjoy doing what everybody else is doing. I would not suggest that many popular hobbies be abandoned merely because one's neighbors are up to the same tricks. But I am suggesting that following the crowd has never really gotten anyone anywhere, except into trouble. So, "in"-keepers of the world, return to the olden days when "in" was an innocent and unsuspecting preposition, meaning what it was intended to mean.

Remember that "in" things invariably become "out" things – and then they become (I swear it) "camp" things. *Camp* means something so bad, so banal and inane – in whose eyes I don't know – that it becomes "in" again. Old comic books are one example. Comic books are not only "in" but they cost more than the first edition of *The Decline and Fall of the Roman Empire*. Perhaps there's some connection.

Anyway, I think it high time we discard "in" and "out" in favor of other prepositions. As for "camp", we should bury it in the deepest hole available. In other words, "in" and "out" will no longer be in or out: in is out, out is out and camp is far out in left field, or whatever it is they say these days.

Now we must choose another preposition, one which will not spread too quickly, for it should be reserved for special people, and special people are simply not to be confused with the masses. One word which appears to reflect the spirit of our times is "up". So, instead of saying in and out, we can start with up and down and see how we fare. In and out already have an old-fashioned ring, and this won't do anymore. They seem to suggest "in and out of traffic"..."in trouble"..."out of breath"..."in heat"..."in winter"...and so on. Such archaic ideas are useless in this super-modern world of computers and jets.

Enter, if you will, the Jet Age, where some things are "up" and others "down". "Up" implies the wind, freedom, flights of fancy. "Down" means time to land or time to go home. So "up" means "in" and "down" means "out", while "down and out" is quite horrible.

Now you can forget your French grammar and stop worrying about how to impress the local insurance salesman at your next party. Now you only have to fly somewhere – or say that you are flying somewhere – to achieve the same effect.

But flying from New York to Waterloo, Missouri, to visit an old aunt, is not enough. This is "out" – I mean, "down". If you really want to be "up", you've got to fly at least eight hours by jet over some strange ocean – then you are definitely "up", not just rising or gaining altitude. "Down" therefore means coming in for a landing, and if you're "up" before coming down, this could mean São Paulo, Singapore or Hongkong. Once is not enough, either – you've got to fly all the time, or *say* that you're flying all the time, even if you can't stand flying in the first place.

Imagine now that you are attending a social gathering at some villa on the Lake of Zurich (Schweiz – Suisse – Svizzera – Switzerland). It's a modest sort of place: forty-four rooms, five or six servants, lots of lovely things to eat and drink – fine French wines and all the rest. Now look carefully, because everybody who is anybody is here tonight – you can tell by the way people are dressed – like old cowpokes back home in the United States! For this is a typical Swiss Zurichsee Barbecue, and the grand old villa on the lake has been transformed into "Alphorn Ranch", and there's plenty of genuine Western music, too. The point here is that while people all over America are trying so hard to act Continental, old Europe is acting cowboyish, with all the fixin's.

My wife and I happened to attend the Alphorn Ranch party and, I must say, it certainly was a humdinger of a blowout. Who would have thought that such things happen on the crystal waters of the Lake of Zurich! Anyway, I was sitting in my freshly pressed cowboy suit at a big long cowboy table (in the most elegant English garden one can imagine) when a woman asked me if I'd ever been to São Paulo (see above for hidden meaning). I told her I hadn't, but that I *had* visited St. Peter's in Rome, and would that do? She gave me a look which was definitely "down" her nose and continued.

She said that she often jetted to São Paulo, but that she preferred Thursdays to Tuesdays, because of some difference in airlines. She said one airline insisted on serving ham with aspic *all* the time. That's why she preferred Thursdays, when she could have her choice of ham or tongue in aspic. But Thursdays, on the other hand, were difficult because of Moochli. Oh, I thought, of course..."Who the devil is Moochli?" I asked.

"Moochli's our dog," she replied. "He gets nervous if I leave him with the butler for more than five days."

"Well, what do you do in such cases?" I inquired.

"No problem," she said. "I just don't stay in São Paulo for more than five days. Then I jet back to Zurich, make sure that Moochli's all right and then whoosh back to meet my husband in Paraguay, where he sells plumbing equipment and billiard tables to the king or whatever they have there."

"But why can't you take Moochli with you on your trips?"

"On our *flights*, you mean? Moochli is much too sensitive to changes of altitude. No, I'd rather return and see that he's happy and enjoying himself, as a good dog should. Then I always jet off again and meet my husband somewhere. You see, the world is our stamping ground and private oyster... *tra-la, tra-la, la-la.*"

I was impressed, and I felt quite unimportant, especially when this important lady told me that she buys her suits in New York, her furs in Paris, her shoes in London and her unmentionables in Moscow. She and her husband own an island in the Aegean, another in Polynesia, and one off of Liverpool, so that they have at least one island wherever they happen to be.

I have since learned that the next step on the way "up" is to have one's own private jet, first a two-engine job, later a full-fledged DC-8 or something. Then you don't have to depend on airlines which serve only ham in aspic. You can have your own genuine Alphorn barbecue way up in the sky above the Indian Ocean... Tuesdays as well as Thursdays, with chicken on Sundays.

The Hostess

Three things preclude my ever becoming an Air Hostess with Swissair. In the first place, I'm not really Swiss. Furthermore, according to the application form I requested, I may be a bit too old for the job. Finally, although one is permitted to be married – which I am – one is not permitted to have children – which I do.

Thus I do not qualify for this fascinating profession, but perhaps another airline will eventually hire me, as I otherwise have quite a lot to offer. At least I think so.

But returning to the original discussion, I am somewhat over forty – about 20% over forty – and Swissair themselves told me that they have had air hostesses – originally called stewardesses – for more than forty years. Now, I thought to myself, if they have had their lovely flying ladies for forty years, some of them must be at least – well, say – fifty-seven or even a little more.

So I called up my old friend at Swissair to complain that somebody was discriminating against me again, for I am capable of being just as friendly and efficient as a Swissair hostess.

"Eugene," he said, "isn't it about time you learned to surmount your old persecution complex?"

"Persecution complex, you say? Whaddya mean,

persecution? All I want to do is apply for a job as an air hostess and you guys right away start thinking up reasons for disqualifying me!"

"Okay, okay, wait a minute. You want to become an air hostess, and you think you can qualify. First of all, you're not really Swiss, right?"

"Well, a lot of people consider me Swiss, and my best friends often compliment me by saying that I think exactly like one – and this makes me very proud."

"All right, now what's next?" my old friend asked. "Ah yes, of course, you're obviously too old. What do you say to that one?"

"You've got me there, Albert! (I call my friend Albert primarily because that's his name.) Except – and listen carefully – I may be over forty, but wouldn't you say, old boy, that if Swissair were to cut both my size and age in half that they could make two air hostesses out of me – at least *intellectually?*"

"Intellectually, let's see now." Albert began looking through one of Swissair's rule books. "I must admit, chum, that it says nothing about intellectualism here. But overlooking this, what about your being married and having children?"

"Albert, you and your whole confederate airline are being eminently unfair with me, and I want you to know that I know it. But I'm willing to forget the whole thing if you'll explain the *real* reason why you don't want me. Come on now, be honest! If it's my breath, I want you to say so. Whatever it is, out with it, we've been friends for long enough."

"Look, Eugene, the most obvious reason you can't become an air hostess has nothing to do with your breath." I heaved a delicate sigh of relief.

He continued. "The best reason I can think of is that you are not a girl. And air hostesses, for some ulterior motive which eludes me, have to be girls. You see, Eugene, you must have overlooked this point when you filled out your application."

"Wait a minute!" I shot back. "There isn't one word in your company's application form that says I have to be a girl. I agree with you that one might surmise as much by defining the term 'air hostess', which is English, and your application form is in German. Now, they ask all kinds of things, such as my telephone number, my education, the languages I speak, whether I can swim, but nowhere do they say I have to be a girl."

Albert shook his disbelieving head from side to side. Then he looked at me with that resigned look of his and asked, "Are you a girl?"

"Hell, no, I'm not a girl! What kind of stupid

question is that? You know darned well I'm thoroughly and completely male – in every chauvinistic way."

"Then why are you giving me such a hard time?"

"I'm giving you a hard time, as you put it, for two reasons, Albert. First of all, I'm for male equality and liberation. If a girl can apply for a job as air hostess with Swissair, then I ought to be able to do the same. Anyway, I like their uniform."

"Eugene, why don't you apply for a job as steward?"

"Ah, here we go again! I don't like to be discriminated against, I said that from the beginning, right?"

"Right," said Albert. "Now what in the name of Helvetia's honor is the other reason you want to be a Swissair hostess? The glamorous life, the hard work, the travel?"

"You really want to know?" I replied.

"No, actually not, but you started the whole thing. So why don't you be a good little boy and tell your favorite Swiss airline why you want to be an air hostess."

"I don't want to be an air hostess. I just wanted to impress you with my sincerity. You see, I certainly would want to be an air hostess if I had the right qualifications. But since I have nothing

to offer – and I'm lazy to boot – I guess I'm simply not the type."

"Go on," Albert suggested. "But wipe the tears
from your eyes first." I started dabbing at my
eyes with some Kleenex I pinched from Swissair
between Athens and Zurich.

"Albert, you and Swissair are right – I don't deserve you. Please keep the standards just as high
as they have been since 1934, when you hired
your first stewardesses. You know, now I remember one particular night in New York –
many years ago. I had waded through snow and
slush to get to the airport and onto the Swissair
plane and I was thoroughly exhausted from two
weeks of wading through snow and slush.

"And as I walked through the door of that
Swissair plane that night, one of your air hostesses, whose name I will never know, smiled
and nodded to me as I entered. All she said was
'Grüezi', but I guess she really made me feel at
home or something. I've been in love with all of
them ever since!"

Draft Aversion

Drafts in restaurants or other public places can cause extremely serious illnesses. I am not sure precisely what illnesses my Swiss friends had in mind when we discussed this question some years ago, but there is no doubt that drafts are pretty awful things.

We were sitting in a pleasant restaurant, enjoying ourselves – at least *I* was enjoying myself – when my friend Walti told the waitress that a terrible draft was blowing from somewhere or other. Ruthli, his wife, thought it emanated from the direction of the kitchen; Walti was certain it came from the opposite direction and was moving *towards* the kitchen. In any case, the kitchen appeared to be of some importance to the discussion. As a matter of fact, the more my friends talked about kitchens, the hungrier I became. I personally think that drafts whet the appetite – at least our private draft helped my appetite that night. But Ruthli and Walti were not yet ready to order any kind of food whatsoever.

"I would like a veal steak *aux morilles*," I ventured, hoping that the mere mention of something edible would encourage thoughts of gastronomic delights. "Or should I begin with some fresh smoked salmon with onions and capers?"

Nothing seemed to work. Walti looked at me and asked how I could possibly think of such capers when there was a definite and unmistakable draft blowing from somewhere.

"All right, all right! I surrender, I give up, and I hereby hold you both responsible for my starving to death in this land of plenty! If drafts cause any illness at all, it's most probably malnutrition!" I was furious. But I had an idea. The only way to settle this matter would be either to find the elusive draft – or simply *not* find it. I strongly believed that there was no draft at all in the immediate vicinity of our table, but I couldn't seem to convince our friends. The obvious solution was to prove it to them – through scientific experiment.

"Walti," I said quietly, "let's examine this situation more closely. Where do you feel the alleged draft, and does it really bother you so much that you and Ruthli are absolutely unable to eat?"

Walti turned to his wife. She pointed to her ankles and then to the back of her neck. She looked terribly uncomfortable. "It's there, I know it's there," she said.

"Perhaps we should change tables," I suggested. "No, that won't do either," said Walti. "In the first place, I like this particular table and, in the second place, there is no second place – all the tables are occupied."

With no choice left, I began my scientific analysis of this complex problem by lighting a candle. "Now examine the flame carefully!" I exclaimed triumphantly. "Notice that it is burning straight and evenly, which it obviously wouldn't do if there were a draft here." I was pleased with my own logic.

Walti shouted back at me. "It's not burning straight at all!" he roared. "Look at it! It's weaving all over the place, like a Sunday driver on his way home from a yodel festival!"

"It's weaving like that," I bellowed back, "because you're shouting at me and the candle at the same time! I'm not afraid of you, Walti, but apparently the candle is. I don't know what kind of man you are, but you shouldn't go around scaring innocent little candles who are only trying to do their thankless job of illuminating restaurant tables and locating occasional drafts. And, speaking of restaurants, how about something to eat? Arguments invariably make me hungry."

"In a minute," Walti answered. "I think we're getting somewhere now." He was examining what appeared to be a pocket watch. "This is a draftometer," he explained. "I forgot I had it with me. Anyway, it never fails to show everything one has to know about assorted winds, breezes and drafts. If there is a window open somewhere, or even the slightest variation in temperature and humidity between this particular room and an inrushing air current, the draftometer will locate it immediately."

At that moment, the draftometer began to ring like an alarm clock. "Watch it closely," said Walti. "All I have to do is follow the direction indicator while it rings and analyze the hygrometric fluctuation from floor to ceiling, and we'll catch this cagey little draft before it can perpetrate any further damage."

"Careful now, slowly now," Walti kept saying to himself as he crept on his hands and knees across the polished floor of the restaurant. He surfaced again at the opposite end of the room. The draftometer was ringing violently, and it also began ticking like a Geiger counter.

"Eureka!" screamed Walti. "Now we have him, somewhere near this table!" He stealthily moved towards the table on tiptoe, ready to pounce as soon as the draftometer gave him the word. "Ready!" he cried as he lunged at the table and into a huge platter of fried fish and mayonnaise. Mayonnaise is easily excited when heavy weights fall into it, and this particular mayonnaise was no exception. It flew in all directions, as did the fried fish – fresh perch from the Lake of Zurich.

Walti emerged beaming. I couldn't recognize

him anymore, but underneath the mayonnaise coating he was holding two objects, one of them ringing, the other bubbling. The draftometer was a greasy mess, but it kept on ringing away. The other object was a plain and simple bottle – nothing more.

I was most embarrassed, probably because of the people at the other table who were still staring at the mess Walti had made of their dinner. "Explain yourself!" I demanded of Walti. "Well," he answered, "the draft really wasn't too serious this time. It came from the carbon-dioxide bubbles escaping from this bottle of mineral water. But at least we found it."

"Carbon dioxide! You have the nerve to sit in this restaurant and hunt carbon-dioxide bubbles? Enough of this gaseous insanity – let's eat already!"

I called the waitress. "What's the specialty tonight?" I asked. "Fried lake perch with mayonnaise," she replied. "And very good, too. Just ask your friend." Walti simply sat there licking mayonnaise off his fingers – and staring lovingly at his draftometer.